D1045118

The Church and the Ecological Crisis

The Church and the Ecological Crisis

by

HENLEE H. BARNETTE

WILLIAM B. EERDMANS PUBLISHING COMPANY
Grand Rapids, Michigan

Copyright © 1972 by William B. Eerdmans Publishing Co.
All rights reserved
Library of Congress Catalog Card No.: 72-77175
ISBN 0-8028-1457-3
Printed in the United States of America

Contents

Preface   7

1. THE ECOLOGICAL ISSUE:
   CRAZE OR CRISIS?   11

2. CAUSATIVE FACTORS IN THE
   ECOLOGICAL CRISIS   27

3. ELEMENTS OF AN ECOLOGICAL ETHIC   35

4. STRATEGIES FOR SURVIVAL   52

5. TOWARD A THEOLOGY FOR ECOLOGY   62

6. THE CHURCH AND THE
   ECOLOGICAL CRISIS   82

   Appendix I: Evil and Nature   92

   Appendix II: "The Theology of Ecology" —
      A Sermon by John R. Claypool   98

   Appendix III: Environmental Societies   108

   Appendix IV: Eco-Films   110

   Appendix V: Bibliography   112

Preface

On Earth Day, April 22, 1970, concern for the environmental crisis reached its emotional peak in America. Across the nation, millions of people demonstrated their concern to save the good earth. School children roamed through communities and picked up tons of trash. In academia, lectures were heard about the ailing ecosystem. Big business proposed — or perhaps announced — the expenditure of millions of dollars to control its own pollution. Politicians got on the anti-pollution bandwagon; indeed, so many Congressmen took part in the Earth Day activities that Congress had to suspend business for that day. Legislators fanned out all over the nation to appear at rallies and teach-ins.

Eco-dramas and demonstrations provided a dramatic touch to the ecological crusade. There were even ecological cartoons: in Johnny Hart's syndicated strip "B-C.," one of the pre-historic characters was shown tasting water from a polluted river. A fellow caveman asked, "What is it?" Reply: "It tastes like progress."

Earth Day grew out of a suggestion by Senator Gaylord Nelson of Wisconsin. Observing the support mobilized by the anti-war effort, he proposed a nationwide "teach-in" on environmental problems. In the days and weeks prior to Earth Day the mass media gave wide coverage to the pollution problem, thus helping to generate emotion and public concern for the ecological crusade.

After Earth Day, public interest in the ecological issue began to wane. The mass media turned their attention to other problems. Why this leveling off of concern for the ecological crisis? For one thing, Americans seem to be a one-problem-per-year people. It is difficult to predict what the "cause-of-the-year" set will be concerned about twelve months from now. Race, poverty, war, sex — and now ecology — have all taken a turn as a national worry.

One major reason for the general cooling toward the ecological issue is not hard to ascertain. Americans are discovering that a cleaner environment will be costly. Removing the poisons accumulated in our natural environment through centuries of thoughtless misuse is expensive, and the consumer will have to foot the bill. This economic factor has tended to diminish emotional fervor for ecological action.

New facts about the ecological problem are surfacing, and a more sober and realistic assessment of the problem has begun to develop. Morever, the average American is becoming aware that he himself is — consciously or unconsciously — a significant contributor to pollution. Yet he is reluctant to change his polluting practices. There is a grim irony in what happened at one institution of higher learning. A newly formed "eco-club" distributed mimeographed materials containing suggestions as to how to de-pollute the environment. Among them was a proposal that one should not use colored tissues, paper towels and the like, due to the pollutant dyes contained therein. The entire list of thirty suggestions was printed on colored paper! As Walt Kelly's cartoon character Pogo has opined: "We have met the enemy and he is us."

Despite the general de-escalation of crusading emotional fervor, ecology will continue to be a major problem for many years. It is more than a passing fad because: (1) a hard core of concerned individuals and groups will continue the struggle against environmental deterioration; (2) environmental control now has built-in aids, among them laws, educational curriculums at every level from kindergarten to the university, and the growing public consciousness of the issue; (3) the growth of organizations concerned with ecology; (4) the shift of the ecology movement from the "alert stage" to political action and from rhetoric to a more accurate analysis; (5) the growing number of scientists and humanists concerned about the health of the environment; (6) the continuing decline of the quality of life due to pollution and overpopulation; and (7) the inseparable relation of the ecological problem to other major and lasting social issues like war, poverty, racism, and population.

In response to the ecological problem, a mountain of literature has appeared, treating it from the scientific, sociological, and historical points of view. Only a few materials are available relating to the theological and ethical perspectives. The aim of these chapters is to summarize the salient factors in the eco-crisis in the light of the biblical understanding of man and nature. Because many churches are striving to become more meaningfully involved in social issues, positively as well as prophetically, it is my intention to pull together facts, figures, and opinions from the vast array of offerings on this subject and put them into a perspective that is helpful for the churchman.

Drawing on the findings of the scientists — particularly the biologists and ecologists — Chapter One presents facts and fallacies about the crisis. Chapter Two is concerned with the roots of the environmental problem, while Chapter Three seeks to articulate an ethic of environmental responsibility. Strategies for survival are suggested in Chapter Four; Chapter Five seeks to formulate a theology for ecology, while Chapter Six suggests practical ways in which the church can help to curb the current ecocidal process and contribute toward a better quality of life in society. The appendices include an attempt to deal with the perplexing problem of Nature and Evil, a model sermon on ecology preached by Dr. John Claypool at Crescent Hill Baptist Church in Louisville, as well as lists of societies, films, and books that will provide further resource material for the concerned reader of this book.

I hope that this book will aid in understanding the problems involved in the area of ecological concerns, and provide a glimmer of hope as well as the beginnings of an answer to the plaintive question "What can *I* do?"

An author is always indebted to many persons. I am grateful to the faculty of Southern Baptist Theological Seminary for inviting me to give the Norton Lectures for the fall of 1971, which form the substance of what appears in this book. Many scholars have contributed to my understanding of the ecological issue. I hope that I will be forgiven for mentioning only Dr. Eric Rust, professor of Christian philosophy, and Dr. Paul Simmons, professor of Christian ethics, both of the Southern Baptist Seminary faculty, and Dr. Wilbur Curless, now pursuing research in biology at the University of Louisville. These three men in particular took the time to dialogue with me about the theological, ethical, and scientific dimensions of the problem. To my wife Helen, who not only typed the first chaotic rough draft, but also made numerous suggestions that improved the style and content of the manuscript, I express my deep appreciation. Jean Aiken typed the final draft and to her I give thanks for her precision and patience in preparing it for the publisher.

— Henlee H. Barnette

DeLand, Florida

1

The Ecological Issue: Craze or Crisis?

We travel together, passengers on a little spaceship, dependent on its vulnerable supplies of air and soil ...preserved from annihilation only by the care, the work ...and the love we give our fragile craft.
— Adlai Stevenson

In 1970 the Apollo 13 spacecraft was damaged in its flight to the moon. During these tense days and nights, special care had to be taken to conserve the resources of the imperiled capsule in order to insure a safe return to the earth. Photographs of our planet taken by astronauts from thousands of miles in space have underscored visually that our planet is a small sphere, limited in resources, closed, whirling through a wilderness of space. Like Apollo 13, our position in the universe is in jeopardy.

Crisis in the Chain of Life

Scientists have long indicated that the earth is surrounded by a thin layer of life known as the biosphere.

The chemical life cycle in this biosphere enables human life to survive. In this life cycle, inorganic elements circulate from environment to organisms and back to the environment. The sum total of the living and nonliving parts that support a chain of life within a given area is called an *ecosystem*. Links in this chain of life are:

(1) Nonliving energy and matter used by plants (sunlight, water, carbon dioxide, and the like).

(2) Plants, which convert by the process of photosynthesis carbon dioxide and water into the carbohydrates that they and other organisms in the system require.

(3) Primary consumers, such as herbivores (cows and sheep, for example), which feed on the producers; and secondary consumers (man and certain animals), which feed on the herbivores.

(4) Decomposers (bacteria, fungi, insects), which complete the cycle of the ecosystem when they break down the dead producers and consumers, returning their chemical compounds to the ecosystem for use again by plants. Any serious disturbance of this chemical life-cycle equilibrium endangers life on earth.

Ecology is the study of the relationship of all living creatures to each other and to their environment. The term comes from the Greek word *oikos,* meaning "house" or "household." Hence, one might say that ecology has to do with the principles and practice of keeping the household of nature in order.[1] Because the study of

---

[1] The Priestly account of creation depicts God as the Great Architect, setting about his task "like an architect intending to build a house." Edmund Jacob, *Theology of the Old Testament* (New York: Harper,

ecology reveals the omni-interdependence of the planet earth, it challenges the human institutions that destroy our natural environment. Therefore it has been called a "subversive science," undermining the big polluters and exploiters of the earth.[2] No longer is ecology viewed merely as a scientific discipline — an obscure branch of biology—but it has become an instrument of social reform.

"Doomsday" scientists hold that the delicate balance between living things and their environment has been so radically upset by irresponsible exploitation and pollution that there is a grave threat to human life as we know it. In apocalyptic rhetoric, these men describe the possible end of civilization. Some have even developed timetables to show that the extinction of mankind is imminent. They predict that if we continue to degrade our environment, such cataclysms as mass starvation and the deluge of a new ice age could occur.[3]

On the other side there are those scientists and businessmen who debunk the notion that man is polluting and populating himself into oblivion. They charge that activists about ecological issues are "ecomaniacs" who sensationalize and overdramatize the ecological problem. Thomas R. Shepard, Jr., former publisher of *Look* magazine, denies that there is any ecological problem at all, much less a crisis. He sees no serious problem with our air, our water, our use of pesticides and detergents, or our growing population. On the contrary, he claims, the environment is becoming cleaner and safer all the time. Ecological activists are, in this view, "the Disaster Lobby." Shepard calls the "Disaster Lobby" the

1958), p. 136. Compare the book of Job, where God exhibits the traits of an architect in marking the land and laying the foundations and the cornerstone of the world.

[2] Paul Shepard and Daniel McKinley, eds., *The Subversive Science* (Boston: Houghton-Mifflin, 1969).

[3] See Gordon Taylor, *The Doomsday Book* (Cleveland: World, 1970); William and Paul Paddock, *Famine 1975! America's Decision: Who Will Survive?* (Boston: Little-Brown, 1967); Paul Ehrlich, *The Population Bomb* (New York: Ballantine, 1970).

most dangerous people in America today. Why? Because they are undermining the free enterprise system. Furthermore, they urge the banning of pesticides and thus threaten death from malaria and other insect-borne diseases to millions of people.[4] Rene Dubos, head of the Department of Environmental Bio-Medicine at Rockefeller University, says he is weary of hearing that extinction is imminent. Actually, he claims, man can adapt to almost anything. Though Dubos is alarmed by the destructive effects of our "power-intoxicated technology" and "ungoverned population growth," he holds that it is not man but his quality of life that is threatened by the ecological crisis.[5]

Somewhere between the radical position of those who see doomsday as around the corner and those who deny that there is any environmental problem at all lies the truth of the matter. There is ample evidence that pollution and population are creating a genuine strain on the carrying capacity of the spaceship earth. An analysis of these problems and the causes for them is essential to developing strategies to maintain the quality of life at as high a level as possible.

Water Pollution

Mother, may I go out to swim?
Yes, my darling daughter;
Hang your clothes on a hickory limb,
But don't go near the water.

The words of this old folk song contain practical advice for today, because most of the water in America has become polluted. Our rivers are rapidly becoming running sewers. Already more than twenty of our major rivers are polluted to the point that fish and other water-life are dying. As a result of pollution, the Mississippi

---

4 "The Disaster Lobby," *IMA* (Chicago: Illinois Manufacturers Association), April, 1971, p. 1.

5 "Guest Privilege," *Life*, July, 1970, p. 2.

River south of St. Louis is so toxic that signs have been erected to warn against eating food grown near its banks. Ohio's Cuyahoga River flowed so thick with oil scum in 1969 that it caught fire, destroying two railroad bridges.

Most of our lakes are threatened by pollution. Twenty years ago I caught fish in abundance from pristine Lake Apopka near Orlando, Florida. Today the lake is dying from poisonous effluents being dumped into it, and fishing there is an exercise in futility. Lake Erie is dying from a discharge of poison at the rate of a ton per minute, and it is in danger of becoming a gigantic swamp.[6] Lake Superior is the last "clean" Great Lake; but this rating will be short-lived, because a mining company is dumping 60,000 long tons of waste directly into it each day.[7]

Water pollution is becoming worldwide. The tidy Swiss are now alarmed to discover that Lakes Geneva and Constance are turning murky from pollutants dumped from lakeside cities and industries. The Rhine River is so toxic that even the eels have difficulty surviving. This is a problem that has been plaguing that river for some time. By 1800, Samuel Taylor Coleridge had already anticipated the problem of pollution there:

> The River Rhine, it is well known
> Doth wash your city of Cologne:
> But tell me, Nymphs, what power divine
> Shall henceforth wash the River Rhine?

Scientists now predict that the Sea of Galilee will be doomed in a decade unless corrective steps are taken to stop the tons of nitrates that flow into it from the heavily planted former marshlands in the Hula region of Israel.

---

[6] Peter Schrag, "Life of a Dying Lake," *Saturday Review*, Sept. 20, 1969, p. 198.

[7] Gaylord Nelson, "This Generation's Strategy to Save the Environment," in *Agenda for Survival*, ed. Harold W. Helfrich, Jr. (New Haven: Yale U.P., 1970), p. 187.

Eventually, polluted streams flow into the oceans that cover 70 percent of the globe. These oceans have vast powers of purification, but they are able to absorb only so much sewage, chemicals, industrial waste, and garbage. When the Norwegian explorer Thor Heyerdahl attempted to sail from Egypt across the Atlantic in a papyrus boat, he and his crew found black lumps of solidified oil and floating debris ever present during their voyage, mute testimonials to man's abuse of his environment hundreds of miles from any human dwelling.

The renowned oceanographer Jacques Cousteau, after returning from a three-and-one-half-year voyage covering 155,000 miles of ocean, declared that the oceans are in danger of dying, that pollution is quite general, and that aquatic life has diminished 40 percent in the last 20 years.[8] Indeed, hardly any part of the oceans along the coasts or coastlines has escaped pollution. Aboard one of the U. S. Navy's deep submersible craft fifty miles off the coast of San Diego and 2,450 feet down, Admiral R. J. Galanso peered through the portholes to view the wonders of the undersea world. The first thing he spotted, only two feet away on the ocean floor, was an empty beer can.[9]

Millions of tons of pollutants consisting of hundreds of different substances annually reach the seas. Sewage, industrial wastes, oil spills, garbage refuse, and chemical runoff from the land threaten the oxygen-producing plants and animals of the sea, without which man cannot survive. Lamont Cole describes pollution of the seas as playing Russian roulette with their chemical life cycles.[10]

8 "The Dying Oceans," *Time*, Sept. 28, 1970, p. 12.

9 Leslie Robinson, *Earth Day — The Beginning* (New York: Bantam Books, 1970), p. 2.

10 "Playing Russian Roulette with Biogeochemical Cycles," in *The Environmental Crisis*, pp. 1-14.

Generally scientists agree that the ocean's future is in jeopardy. While the prediction of ecologist Paul Ehrlich that all important life in the sea may be doomed by 1979[11] may be greatly exaggerated, what Lord Byron wrote a century and a half ago can no longer be said:

> Roll on, thou deep and dark blue ocean — roll!
> Ten thousand fleets sweep over Thee in vain;
> Man marks the earth with ruin — his control
> Stops with the shore.

Man not only "marks" the earth by his ruthless exploitation — now he has violated the sea, and the wounds are quite visible to the human eye.

Air Pollution

Clean air is essential for man's health. The average person breathes about 35 pounds of air — this mixture of nitrogen and oxygen gases indispensable to human life — each day. Man cannot go without air for more than six minutes without suffering some degree of brain damage. But our air is no longer clean. More than 3,000 foreign chemicals have been identified in the atmosphere; more than 140 million tons of pollutants are put into the air each year over the United States.[12]

Most large cities have serious air pollution problems. A scientific analysis of New York City's atmosphere concluded that the toxic material inhaled into the lungs of the average man on the streets of that city is equivalent to 38 cigarettes per day.[13] Los Angeles is notorious for its smog, which causes stinging eyes and sometimes illness. On days when the pollution reaches a certain

11 "Eco-Catastrophe!" in *The Environmental Handbook,* ed. Garrett DeBell (New York: Ballantine, 1970), p. 174.

12 Paul and Anne Ehrlich, *Population, Resources, Environment* (San Francisco: Freeman, 1970), p. 119.

13 Robert and Leona Rienow, *Moment in the Sun* (New York: Ballantine, 1967), pp. 141ff.

density, school children must be restrained from participating in gym classes due to excessive strain on the body. From 25,000 miles in space the Apollo 10 astronauts easily identified the City of the Angels as a smudge of smoke. Airline pilots maintain that from a distance of 70 miles a brown shroud of pollution can be seen around almost very major city in the United States.

In August 1970, a sulphurous haze hung over the Atlantic coast from Washington to New York. One could barely spot the Capitol Building from the Washington Monument. New Yorkers suffered with stinging eyes and sore throats. Some were hospitalized. The sulfur dioxide level soared to 0.23 parts per million, nearly twice the unhealthy level. This situation was caused by an atmospheric "thermal inversion." In this phenomenon, the air at higher levels is warmer than that at lower levels and shuts off the upward flow of air, sealing deadly pollutants into the lower atmosphere. Thermal inversions have happened often in Los Angeles, New York, and other cities, and they are occurring with increasing frequency.

Like water pollution, air pollution too is a worldwide concern. In Tokyo, thousands of residents have been hospitalized in recent years because of what they breathe. Many people there never venture out of doors without white gauze masks. Oxygen-vending machines have become common, providing whiffs of fresh air for twenty-five cents.[14]

Death rates among the very old, the very young, and those with respiratory diseases are above normal where smog occurs. Chronic asthma, bronchitis, and emphysema have a high incidence where there is severe air pollution.[15]

[14] "Here Comes the Smog," *Newsweek*, Aug. 10, 1970, p. 64.
[15] Paul and Anne Ehrlich, *op. cit.*, pp. 119-123.

Noise Pollution

Another kind of pollution plaguing modern man is noise pollution. The "environmental din" is doubling each decade, so that there is hardly a quiet spot left on earth. Air compressors and jackhammers, televisions and radios, jets, autos, and motorcycles confront man everywhere. Thoreau may have found quiet at Walden Pond, but almost every lake today is filled with the roar of outboard motors and surrounded by concession stands and motels. Snowmobiles and their 700,000 owners emerge in the winter to disturb the quiet of the snow-covered plains and hills. Dune buggies bounce over sun-splashed beaches. Over and above all the noise we hear every day we can look forward to the sonic boom of the supersonic transport (SST), scheduled to start flights in the next four years. In addition to these man-made sounds, there are the throbbing waves of "silent sound" that bathe the earth and cause us to be nervous and irritable. These "infrasonics" are produced by phenomena like earthquakes, storms, and explosions.

Noise is measured in terms of decibels, a unit of relative noise intensity. Silence represents zero decibels; ten decibels has the intensity of rustling leaves. At the other end of the spectrum is the sound of a jet plane at takeoff, which amounts to 150 decibels. Rock music throbbing through amplifiers is measured at 110 decibels. According to the American Medical Association, any noise registering over 85 decibels is harmful if the listener has prolonged exposure.

John Handey, an authority on industrial acoustics, states that research on the effects of noise on people suggests that noise pollution may be one of the reasons for the high incidence of heart disease and mental illness in this country. Other authorities think that stomach ulcers, allergies, enuresis, excessive cholesterol, indigestion, and even impaired vision may be due to noise.[16] Otologist Samuel Rosen observes that noise cannot be shut out from the ear as light can be from the eyes, so that the reflex effect that causes restriction of blood vessels occurs with equal intensity during sleep as when one is awake.[17]

In the face of all this, however, modern man appears to be developing an addiction to noise. As one writer puts it, man is "getting hooked on the stuff," for many people need the escapist blare of canned or live music before they can function adequately.[18] Silence is frightening to man; he is fearful of the sound of nothing or, as the popular song puts it, "the Sounds of Silence."

Noise abatement programs are rare. The public is simply unaware of the damaging effects of noise. The U. S. government is doing almost nothing about noise abatement. The Health, Education and Welfare Department has little in its program to curb noise pollution, even though this malady seems to be a significant contributor to ill health in the nation. Private groups are just beginning to confront the problem.

Poison Pollution

Since the publication of Rachel Carson's *Silent Spring* in 1962, pesticides have been the subject of vigorous debate. Dr. Carson's warning that DDT is dangerous to plants, animals, and human beings led pesticide manufacturers to seek to ban publication of her book. Today, after ten years of controversy the book has been vindicated as a warning of the dangers of pesticides; and the American people now see the need to save their environment from destruction by chemical poisoning.[19]

[16] John M. Mecklin, "It's Time to Turn Down All That Noise," in *The Environment* (New York: Harper, 1970), p. 137.

[17] *Quiet!* (New York: Citizens for a Quieter City), No. 1 (Spring 1969), p. 1.

[18] William Zinsser, "Are We Hooked on Noise?," *Life,* Oct. 31, 1970, p. 12.

[19] See Frank Graham, Jr., *Since Silent Spring* (Boston: Houghton-

There is a large amount of evidence indicating that pesticides kill birds, animals, and fish and other marine life as well as pests. The Department of the Interior has issued a list of 101 species of animals, birds, and fish that face extinction; twenty-two of those recently added to the list are said to be threatened mainly from pollution, especially pesticides, or by destruction of their habitat. Studies have shown that when certain birds ingest pesticides, the eggs they lay are thin-shelled and do not protect the embryo. The osprey, the brown pelican, and the Bermuda petrel are among the birds declining in population due to this "thin-shelled phenomenon."[20]

Some have argued that this is no real cause for concern, since hundreds of species of animals, birds, and fish have become extinct since the time of recorded history, only to be replaced by new forms. This is true when the species die through natural means. But when they are killed off quickly by other than natural means, no new forms appear in their place. Hence, every species exterminated or killed off represents a complete loss.[21]

DDT and products like it also harm — and sometimes kill — human beings. According to the Food and Drug Administration, between eight hundred and a thousand people die each year from pesticide poisoning and another 85,000 are injured.[22] DDT and other chlorinated hydrocarbon compounds also threaten the oceanic food

Mifflin, 1970). DDT was first synthesized by a German chemist in 1874, but its properties as an insecticide were not discovered until 1939. Hailed as a harmless pesticide, it was first used by soldiers, refugees, and prisoners during World War II to kill lice.

[20] See Charles F. Wurster, "DDT and Environment," in *Agenda for Survival*, ed. Harold W. Helfrich, Jr. (New Haven: Yale U.P., 1970), pp. 37-54.

[21] Vinzenz Ziswiler, *Extinct and Vanishing Animals*, rev. Eng. ed. trans. Fred and Pille Bunnell (New York: Springer Verlag New York, Inc., 1967), p. 56.

[22] Steven H. Wodka, "Pesticides Since Silent Spring," in *Environmental Handbook*, p. 76.

chain by their adverse effects on photosynthesis in algae. There is also some evidence of possible genetic effects on insects, animals, and human beings.

Chemical pesticides have penetrated into the tissue of living creatures all over the world. DDT has been detected in penguins in Arctic regions. The ingestion of DDT by infants is almost twice the daily amount allowable according to maximum standards recommended by the World Health Organization. In the United States, according to Paul and Anne Ehrlich, "most mother's milk contains so much DDT that it would be declared illegal in interstate commerce if it were sold as cow's milk."[23]

Other poisons such as nuclear radiation, mercury, and acid runoff from strip mining and industry threaten living creatures and their environment. Tests of nuclear weapons pollute the biosphere with possible effects on the thyroid glands of children. Underground nuclear tests and nuclear power stations will increasingly expose man to radiation. Consequently there will be genetic risks and possible harmful effects on the human embryo and fetus. More effective methods for controlling radiation and disposing of radioactive wastes must be developed.

Mercury contamination of fish is now well documented. Tests throughout the United States reveal that in some lakes and rivers the levels of mercury are higher than .5 part per million, the point the Food and Drug Administration considers to be dangerous. Phosphates dumped into rivers and lakes can cause eutrophication (overfertilization) of algae, leading to the formation of the green scum that is seen on lakes all across the nation. These algae blooms deplete the oxygen in the water, thus killing off fish and other marine life.

Herbicides (weed-killing chemicals) also pose a threat

[23] *Op. cit.*, p. 129.

to man's health and environment. Such defoliants and herbicides as 2,4,5-T are used on food crops, and the chemical 2,4-D marked "potentially dangerous" is widely applied to corn and wheat crops. The massive military use of herbicides by the United States in an effort to denude the jungle sanctuaries of the Viet Cong in South Vietnam may have caused serious long-range damage to this land and people.[24] Published stories and pictures of the defoliation effort reveal vast and perhaps permanent destruction of mangrove forests. Six years after spraying such areas, the vegetation has not grown back. News accounts indicate also the possibility that the use of herbicides is causing birth malformations among infants of exposed mothers. Stories of this have been suppressed by the Thieu government as "interfering with the war effort," but not denied. A study by the American Association for the Advancement of Science reveals a rise in defective births in South Vietnam since the heavy spraying of herbicides began in 1966. Though a conclusive connection was not established between the two, there is considerable evidence that there is a correlation between the increase in the number of defective births and the massive spraying of herbicides.

Eco-backlash

Since the ecology movement strikes at the economic forces that cause pollution and degradation of our environment, we are witnessing at the present time an inevitable eco-backlash. Editors of certain papers, some government officials, and business representatives are seeking to discredit the findings of the ecologists and other scientists. "Don't listen to the Doomsayers" is typical advice from some editors and syndicated columnists. They argue that family size should be a matter of free choice, that there are people in other countries with

24 See Barry Weisberg, *Ecocide in Indo-China: The Ecology of War.*

denser populations who live a good life, and that the United States has millions of acres of unoccupied land. What they completely overlook is that even if population does not increase in this country, pollution *will* continue to increase because of increased levels of consumption and production.

Another common argument centers around the revelation that tuna samples caught between 1878 and 1909 and preserved in the Smithsonian Institute contained a greater concentration of mercury than tuna recently caught off the coast of California. This is supposed to prove that there is no mercury problem and to exonerate industries that are dumping mercury into our streams, lakes, and oceans. But scientists have shown that the increased mercury content in a Greenland ice sheet is evidence of recent input by man.[25]

A pressure group financed by road builders and other highway interests is dispatching "truth squads" to discredit the ecology movement. The "road gang," as they are known around Washington, wants to build more superhighways to accommodate greater motor vehicle production, which will mean higher fuel consumption. Conveniently ignored is any thought of responsibility for the rape of the countryside that this involves.

Political expediency has rendered government control of pollution and poisons less than effective. The official ban on DDT in 1970 was full of loopholes. While the Agriculture Department has canceled and suspended a number of registered uses for DDT and certain pesticides, the government balks at a more rigorous ban on their use. This in spite of the fact that a panel of scientists reported to W. D. Ruckelshaus, the Environmental Protection Agency Administrator, that the current levels of the use of DDT and related pesticides present a substantial threat to human beings and their environment.

[25] "Mercury in a Greenland Ice Sheet: Evidence of Recent Input by Man," *Science*, Nov. 12, 1971, pp. 692-694.

Recently U. S. Surgeon General Jessie L. Steinfeld urged reconsideration of state and local laws banning or restricting the use of phosphates in detergents. He maintains that phosphates are safer than NTA and other substitutes and advises housewives to go back to using phosphate detergents. Representatives of eleven environmental and consumer organizations and the director of the Food and Drug Administration's Bureau of Product Safety criticized Steinfeld's advice as unsound. It is hoped that his advice will not delay efforts to discover alternatives to phosphates in detergents.

Perhaps some ecologists have engaged in exaggerated rhetoric. But an "alert-stage" was essential for awakening people to the crisis. The findings of numerous scientists agree — on the basis of research, not vested interests — that there is a genuine environmental problem that threatens the quality of man's life on a worldwide scale. Indeed, the issue is so great that the United Nations plans to convene in Stockholm in June 1972 delegates from 130 nations for a planet-wide look at the environment.

Meanwhile, the debate about the health of our environment goes on. Since there are scientists who claim that there is no ecological crisis, should we even be concerned? It should be noted in the first place that such studies have largely been undertaken for persons or groups with vested interests in business, government, and the military. We know that we are being buried under scrapped cars (7 million a year), waste paper (30 million tons a year), discarded cans (40 billion a year), and bottles and jars (20 billion a year); that the air is filled with pollutants; and that the fish and marine life are dying in the rivers, lakes, and oceans.

Sober scientists with no vested interests assert that we must stop degrading our environment or we will soon be "ecological orphans." These scientists are pessimistic about man's will to save the world from ecological disaster. They do not lightly dismiss the possibility of an apocalyptic end of civilization. Others agree that there is an environmental dilemma, but they remain optimistic that a higher quality of life on earth can be achieved. They understand "crisis" to mean what it does in the Chinese language: danger and opportunity. Though the ecological problem has reached a dangerous level, they see an opportunity to reverse or at least to control the ecocidal process. Therefore, they reject the notion that since we are on a sinking ship, we might as well go first class.

2

Causative Factors in the Ecological Crisis

"We have met the enemy and he is us."
— Pogo

The ecological problem is an extremely complex and many-faceted issue. It is a fallacy to suppose that one single "cause" of it can be identified. The aim of this chapter is to point out and describe some of the underlying cultural and technical factors contributing to the environmental crisis.

Anthropocentrism

Some argue that the ecological crisis stems from the anthropocentric philosophy of Western man, which sees man at the center of all created values, with the right and responsibility to exploit nature for his own purposes and ends. The attempt is often made to explain this exploitative attitude on the basis of the Judeo-Christian tradition. It is argued that this tradition teaches the superiority of man to all other creation, which he is to

27

use for his pleasure and profit. The prooftext most often cited for this view is found in the Old Testament: "Be fruitful and multiply, and fill the earth and subdue it; and have dominion over the fish of the sea and over the birds of the air and over every living thing that moves upon the earth" (Gen. 1:28).

Ian McHarg, landscape architect and ecologist, maintains that this passage in Genesis, with its stress on man's dominion and subjugation of nature, encourages "the exploitative and destructive instincts in man."[1] He contends that if one were to seek a license to "increase radioactivity, create canals and harbors with atomic bombs, employ poisons without constraint, or give consent to the bulldozer mentality, there could be no better injunction than this text."[2] The biblical view of man, McHarg warns, is "a fantasy . . . and the best guarantee of his extinction."[3] Like McHarg, Dr. Lynn White, Jr., traces the ecological crisis back to Genesis 1:28. White holds that Christianity has become "the most anthropocentric religion the world has ever seen."[4]

White thinks that the animists of antiquity were better ecologists than many Christians, for the animists saw that natural objects — brooks, trees, mountains — possessed guardian spirits that men sought to placate before they trespassed on their domain or utilized their resources. But destroying pagan animism enabled man to become indifferent to nature and to devastate the environment, often claiming biblical sanction for doing so. Thus White sees the Judeo-Christian understanding of the relationship between man and nature as anti-ecological, in that it sees a basic indifference — even antagonism — between them. Present scientific practice and technology, he says, are so tinctured with Christian arro-

---

[1] "The Plight," in *The Environmental Crisis*, p. 25.

[2] *Ibid.*

[3] Quoted in the Louisville *Times*, Sept. 25, 1970, p. A-8.

[4] "The Historical Roots of the Ecologic Crisis," *Science*, Mar. 10, 1967, pp. 1205ff.

gance toward nature that "more of the same" will not solve the ecological crisis. The roots of the problem are largely religious, and the remedy must therefore be essentially religious. He suggests that the solution is to recapture the reverent attitude that the thirteenth-century Franciscan monks held toward nature. St. Francis, who founded the Franciscan Order, recognized the spiritual autonomy of all parts of nature and spoke of Brother Sun, Sister Moon, Brother Wind, and Sister Earth, each of whom praised the Creator in his own way. Hence White nominates Francis as the patron saint of ecology.

Both McHarg and White appear to have fallen into the trap of seeking — and presuming to find — a one-cause theory to explain the ecological problem. We shall deal with the "prooftexting" of this approach in Chapter Five; suffice it to say here that both overlook the Genesis passage that tells that God placed man in the Garden to dress and to keep it (2:15). Both build their cases on *one* passage of scripture; and to make it even more inexcusable, they misinterpret that passage.

Nor is it the case that only Christians are guilty of environmental misuse. The non-Christian Chinese, Greeks, and Romans all contributed to deforestation, erosion, and general devastation of nature. Exploitation of nature has characterized most nations and peoples who have ever inhabited the earth. It is true that animists are less likely indiscriminately to destroy nature for fear of incurring reprisals from the spirits. However, as Professor Lewis Moncrief observes, the fact that another culture does not see spiritual beings in natural objects does not mean that it will ruthlessly exploit its resources. Rather it simply means that there are fewer restraints, psychological and social, against such action.[5]

Rene Dubos feels that St. Benedict would be a better choice as the "patron saint of ecology" than St. Francis.

5 "The Cultural Basis for Our Ecological Crisis," *Science,* Oct. 30, 1970, p. 509.

Benedict founded the first great monastery in the Western world on Monte Cassino, Italy, in the sixth century. Among his regulations was a provision that monks should not only pray but also work and become self-sufficient. Among other things, the monks learned to manage the land in such a way that it both supplied them with food and retained its productivity. In addition, these monks developed an architecture, both functional and beautiful, which was well suited to their locale. Dubos concludes that St. Benedict's rules are more relevant to the ecological problem today than is the worshipful attitude of St. Francis.[6]

Technology

Western technology had its simple beginnings in water and wind power. From efforts to utilize these natural elements, ingenious developers have moved from crude inventions to complex machinery, labor-saving devices, and giant computers. Technology has become the handmaid of science and has made it possible for man to solve many baffling problems and to exploit nature. At the same time, technology is producing some undesirable products that pollute the environment. One of the bad results is overutilization of natural resources for nonessential products. Natural resources are being extracted from the earth at a frightening rate without replenishment. Many nonrenewable minerals are being used up rapidly.

In the current debate about the urgency of the ecological crisis, two opposing views of the role of technology have arisen. *Technophiles* hold that science and technology can solve the problems of resources and the pollution crisis. Dazzled by the feats of technology, they have faith in its limitless power to solve all problems and to

[6] *A Theology of the Earth* (Washington, D.C.: Smithsonian Institute, 1969).

save mankind. *Technophobes,* on the other hand, tend to see technology as an evil force, an "anti-christ" that has led to the current ecological crisis.[7]

In the meantime, technology continues to mushroom and its results become more widespread. The Slussers describe this phenomenon graphically:

> Every year a million or so acres fall before the bull-dozer and become a part of the urban sprawl. Acres of farmland, swamp, field, and forests disappear. Swamps and marshes are filled, hills are leveled, replacing the natural look of the landscape with a product of the engineering mind-set. Highways, airports, houses, streets, sidewalks, factories, warehouses — all rush to claim the land. Trees and grass, hills and streams, are rapidly becoming things confined to areas set aside as nature "museums," where often it is necessary to pay admission to view them. Our landscape is being brutalized by a philosophy which says, "Because it can be built at a profit, it should be built."[8]

Where will it all end? Certainly no rational person would reject — or could *reject* — all technology and insist on returning to a pre-technological age. But it is clear that technology must be tamed and become an instrument for the improvement rather than the destruction of our environment.

Consumerism

With 6 percent of the world's population, the United States consumes approximately 50 percent of the world's resources. One estimate is that 25 tons of minerals are taken from the earth and processed each year to support

[7] For in-depth studies of the optimism/pessimism issue of technology, see Jacques Ellul, *The Technological Society* (New York: Knopf, 1964); Ian G. Barbour, *Science and Secularity* (New York: Harper, 1970); Barry Commoner, *The Closing Circle* (New York: Knopf, 1971).

[8] *Technology — the God That Failed* (Philadelphia: Westminster, 1971), p. 150.

every single American. In many instances, resources are being used up without being replaced. At the present rate of consumption, for example, the nation will be using more trees in 1980 than it can grow.[9]

Consumerism is directly related to pollution. The average American produces almost six pounds of solid waste each day, or more than a ton per year. The amount of resources used by an American will vary according to his affluence; Paul Ehrlich estimates that the average white, middle-class American baby has a future consumption and pollution fifty times greater than that of a baby born in Calcutta, India.[10]

In such a consumer culture, hidden persuaders manipulate the consumer into buying what is really nonessential. (Who actually *needs* a water mattress, a life-sized teddy bear, or a sealskin coat?) Nor is this effect limited to "straight," middle-class society. Often the environmentally concerned "hippie" will spend considerable money on the trappings of the allegedly simple life style. The well-stocked shelves and high turnover in stores dealing in the "hippie trade" are interesting evidence that consumerism is rife even among the nonconformists. Vance Packard has exposed the systematic effort of the business community to encourage Americans to develop buying habits that turn consumers into wasteful, debt-ridden, and permanently discontented persons — all of it under the guise of "keeping America strong."[11] Consumption for consumption's sake is debilitating at every level.

The hidden and not-so-hidden persuaders encourage the throwaway spirit in a throwaway society. The waste makers have developed the technique of "planned obsolescence" whereby consumer goods are deliberately

9 "Special Report: Turning Junk and Trash into a Resource," *Business Week,* Oct. 10, 1970, p. 65.

10 "Playboy Interview: Dr. Paul Ehrlich," *Playboy,* August 1970.

11 *The Waste Makers* (New York: Pocket Books, 1968).

made in an inferior manner so that they will break down or wear out in a short time and require that a replacement be purchased. The market is glutted with non-essentials and inferior products. To end this glut, the marketing experts encourage gluttony.[12] In short, the aim is to develop spending on the basis of want rather than of need.

Overpopulation

Approximately three and one-half billion people are now living on planet earth, with seventy million being added each year. According to U. S. Census Director George Hay Brown, the world's population will double by the year 2000, despite slower growth rates in industrialized nations. The Census Bureau projects a total population of nearly 390 million in the United States by A.D. 2020.

These increases in the population will be an enormous drain on the earth's natural resources and food supply, and will further complicate the already intolerable pollution problem. Consider the potential burden of *one* newborn baby on the environment:

> Every eight seconds a new American is born. He is a disarming little thing, but he begins to scream loudly in a voice that can be heard for seventy years. He is screaming for fifty-six million gallons of water, 21 thousand gallons of gasoline, 10,150 pounds of meat, 28,000 pounds of milk and cream, 9,000 pounds of wheat, and great storehouses of all other foods, drinks, and tobaccos. These are his lifetime demands of his country and its economy.
>
> He is requisitioning a private endowment of 5,000 to 8,000 dollars for school building materials, $6,300 worth of clothing, $7,000 worth of furniture — and 210 pounds of peanuts to pass through his hot, grasping little hand. Yet he is yelping for a Paul Bunyan

12 *Ibid.,* p. 25.

chunk, in his own right, of the nation's pulpwood, paper, steel, zinc, magnesium, aluminum, and tin.

He is heralded as a prodigious consumer in a nation that accounts for one-fourth of the earth's people but consumes half its total product. In one year we use up enough big trees to build a ten-foot boardwalk thirty times around the world at the equator.[13]

Since human population is increasing at an exponential rate, some ecologists predict mass starvation toward the end of the 1970s. By this time, Paul Ehrlich thinks, the world will be plagued by families in which hundreds of millions of people will starve to death despite any crash programs initiated now.[14] Ehrlich is convinced that such schemes as shipping our surplus population to other planets, feeding the world from the resources of the ocean, and the "Green Revolution" will not solve the food problem.[15] Already half the people of the world are undernourished or malnourished. The only realistic solution to the problem is to reduce world population.

Anthropocentrism, technology, consumerism and population growth are some of the major contributing factors to the environmental crisis. The entire blame cannot be placed upon any one factor such as industry or business. The onus of the pollution problem rests upon individuals as well as corporate entities. All are bound up in a solidarity of sin — the sin of degrading nature.

To cope with the factors that contribute to the environmental problem, man needs ethical guidelines. To such ethical principles of action we shall turn in the next chapter.

13 Robert and Leona Rienow, *Moment in the Sun* (New York: Ballantine, 1967), p. 3.

14 *The Population Bomb* (New York: Ballantine, 1968), p. 20.

15 "Famine, 1975: Fact or Fallacy?," in *The Environmental Crisis*, pp. 54-62.

3

Elements of an Ecological Ethic

No important change in ethics was ever accomplished without an internal change in our intellectual emphasis, loyalties, affections, and convictions. The proof that conservation has not yet touched these foundations of conduct lies in the fact that philosophy and religion have not yet heard of it.

— Aldo Leopold

Historically, ethicists have limited the scope of moral responsibility almost wholly to man and society. Forty years ago Albert Schweitzer noted that the "great fault of ethics hitherto has been to deal only with man's relations to man."[1] Twenty-five years ago, Aldo Leopold, noted ecologist, complained that there was "no ethic dealing with man's relation to the land and to the animals and plants which grow upon it."[2] But a dictionary of Christian ethics published only five years ago, which claims to cover the whole field of Christian ethics past

[1] *Out of My Life and Thought* (New York: Holt, 1933), p. 133.
[2] *Sand County Almanac* (New York: Oxford U.P., 1966), p. 218.

and present, still has no entry on the subject of ecology.[3]

In the light of the ecological crisis, it is imperative that the zone of ethics be extended to man in his total environment. Ethics must be redefined to include man not only in relation to his neighbor and the social order, but in his relation to all creatures and things, the organic and the inorganic. This chapter will attempt briefly to set forth some basic elements of an ecological ethic.

Agape *as the Norm of an Eco-ethic*

If we are to develop our ecological ethic from the Christian perspective, we will take note of both faith and facts. We will look to the sciences for the facts of social reality — for *what is* — and to the norms of revelation for *what ought to be*. This mating of faith and fact in the environmental situation will require a multiple perspective, an interdisciplinary approach to the ecological dilemma. The results of this interdisciplinary approach will be brought together into a principle of judgment and action that is coherent and normative.

Agape is the basic normative principle of judgment and action. This agapeic love means to will the welfare of all living creatures and things. It is grounded in God, whose being is love (I John 4:8) ; and it extends, as does God's love, to the whole creation. God so loved the world that all men may have life and have it in abundance (John 3:16; 10:10). Love constrains us not only to will the welfare of our neighbor, but also to preserve and promote the kind of environment that maximizes the possibility of full selfhood for each.

God's will of love brought the universe into being. This is the basis for our accepting that creation as good, as something that has value in itself. It follows then,

3 John Macquarrie, ed., *Dictionary of Christian Ethics* (Philadelphia: Westminster, 1967).

Langdon Gilkey says, that "the products of this will must exist for fulfillment, and not for mockery and destruction."[4] The world is God's sanctuary. In it his creative will of love is at work as history moves to its final goal. The world is the bearer of the holy. Ruthlessly to rape and degrade it violates God's creative love.

Agape, in the sense of willing the welfare of all creatures and things, is the basic principle of human behavior. But if this love is to find concrete expression in relation to the environmental problem, we must look at some ethical elements that illuminate and implement love more precisely. To these we turn now.

A Holistic Ethic

If love wills the welfare of all creation, its scope must be holistic, touching all the relationships of man with his environment. Some ecologists have distinguished between autecology (the study of individual species) and synecology (the study of all the environmental interrelationships of an ecosystem). Applying these terms to ethics, Paul Harrison observes that Christian ethics has been "autethical" rather than "synethical," and so it has tended to focus, as scientists and technologists do, on particulars.[5] Christian ethics must take the synethical approach, and see man's life as bound up with the whole creation. Man does not stand outside of, but lives in solidarity with nature. A Christian ecological ethic, then, will take into account the total context of all that exists.

Both biblical and biological views of nature see the interconnection and interdependence of man and his environment. Man is so intrinsically related to nature that when he sins against God, nature suffers; and when he obeys God, nature rejoices. Biologists know that man is utterly dependent on nature and the chemical chain

[4] *Maker of Heaven and Earth* (Garden City, N.Y.: Anchor Books, 1965), p. 273.
[5] "The Ecological Approach," *The Alumni Bulletin*, Bangor Theological Seminary, Spring 1970, pp. 16-17.

of life. He cannot accomplish what the smallest micro-organism can, namely photosynthesis. Without the oxygen-producing animals and plants, man simply cannot exist. But plants and animals cannot survive if man is bent on destroying them by polluting the ecosystems.

Everything is related to everything else in the universe in an intricate system of plants, animals, micro-organisms, space, planets, stars, wind, and water. That which affects one affects the other, though imperceptibly to the human eye. The poet Francis Thompson puts it this way:

> *All things by immortal power*
> *Near and far*
> *Hiddenly*
> *To each other linkèd are,*
> *Thou canst not stir a flower*
> *Without troubling of a star.*
>   ("The Mistress of Vision")

An Ethic of Adoration

An ecological ethic calls for recovery of a sense of adoration of nature. This is clearly a biblical theme, rooted in a consciousness of God's presence in the world (Ps. 19:1). But man in today's technostructured society does not contemplate nature long enough to see God's witness there. "When nature ceases to be an object of contemplation and admiration," says Albert Camus, "it can then be nothing more than material for an action that aims at transforming it." When man is uprooted from nature, God is expelled from history, and man becomes a despoiler of and alien to his environment.[6]

Paul Santmire detects a kind of schizophrenia in the attitude of Americans toward nature: on the one hand there is adoration of it; on the other, exploitation. The roots of this contradiction lie on the one side in the

---

[6] Camus, *The Rebel* (New York: Random House, 1962), pp. 299-300.

traditional nineteenth-century Western theme of "Nature over Civilization," which became obsessive in some quarters, developing into a romanticized ethic of adoration of nature and aversion to machines and cities. But in the same century, the theme of "Civilization over Nature" became obsessive among others, and this developed into an ethic of exploitation of nature for the sake of "progress," resulting in the devastation of the environment. The twentieth-century counterpart of the ethic of adoration is the cult of the simple rustic life that prompts some Americans to turn away from the social challenges of the city. The ethic of exploitation, on the other hand, has its contemporary counterpart in the cult of manipulation that has caused many Americans to disregard the rights of nature.[7]

Man needs both nature and technological progress. But he can have both only if he looks on the empirical world with a sense of wonder and utilizes it with a sense of moral responsibility. Loren Eiseley well expresses the attitude man must develop toward nature before he is likely to become a responsible steward of his environment:

> I want to look at this natural world both from the empirical point of view and from one which also takes into account that sense of awe and marvel which is a part of man's primitive heritage, and without which man would not be man. . . . For many of us the biblical bush still burns, and there is a deep mystery in the heart of a simple seed.[8]

An Ethic of Reverence for Life

Another element of an ecological ethic is an attitude of reverence for all life. Albert Schweitzer has made a significant contribution in this direction. The philosophical basis of his ethic is that all living things have

---

[7] Paul Santmire, *Brother Earth* (New York: Nelson, 1970), Chapter 1.
[8] *The Firmament of Time* (New York: Atheneum, 1967), p. 8.

"a will to live." The individual human being has a will-to-live among other "wills-to-live," which takes one "back to the mysterious movements of life as it is in itself."[9] Schweitzer's ethics thus embrace man's attitude toward all of life, whether it flourishes in his backyard or on the other side of the world. No man is fully ethical, concludes Schweitzer, unless all of life is sacred to him, "that of plants and animals as that of his fellow-man."[10]

An Ethic of Sympathy for Nature

Sympathy for nature in her agony is another ethical attitude essential for a healthy relationship to one's environment. The Apostle Paul declares that all creation groans as a woman in labor as it awaits redemption (Rom. 8:19-23). Man's sin against God pulled nature down along with man. God's curse fell on the earth. As a result, the Old Testament teaches, all of nature is gripped in the mystery of pain and waits in hope for redemption (Isa. 65:17ff.). This same expectation appears in the New Testament (II Pet. 3:13; Rev. 21:1). Creation, therefore, will share in man's redemption.

Paul Tillich is one of the few recent theologians who showed an appreciation for nature in her suffering. In a sermon entitled "Nature, Also, Mourns for a Lost Good," he expresses a tender concern for nature in her agony. Tillich sees that man, in his technical civilization, has lost the ability to live with nature. As a result, he has occupied everything for domination and ruthless exploitation. Subjugated to these destructive and despoiling tendencies, nature is suffering and sighing along with man himself. Thus the tragedy of nature and of man are bound up together and the salvation of nature is dependent upon the salvation of man. Since man

9 *Civilization and Ethics* (London: A. and G. Black, 1929), p. 216.
10 *Ibid.*, p. 126.

is estranged from nature he must become reconciled with it, listen to it, and then it will not only sigh with him but speak of the hope of salvation.[11]

An Ethic of Thou-ness

The Jewish philosopher Martin Buber has distinguished between two fundamental attitudes toward beings and things in the world: respect and exploitation. These attitudes are represented by what Buber calls the I-Thou and I-It relations respectively. Every man lives in the twofold I. The I-Thou is characterized by mutuality, directness, ineffability. The I-It is subjective and lacking in mutuality, a subject-object relationship. The Thou of the I-Thou is not limited to persons, and may also include animals, trees, objects of nature, and God. The It of the I-It may well be a he, a she, an animal, a thing, a spirit, or even God.[12]

Here is a clue for an ecological ethic. Modern man tends to look at the world as an It. The I-It is not evil in itself, but it becomes so when it is allowed to have mastery and allows man to escape the realm of the I-Thou. And, Buber says,

> In our age the I-It relation is gigantically swollen, has usurped, practically uncontested, the mastery and the rule. The I of this relation, an I that possesses all, makes all, succeeds with all, this I unable to say Thou, unable to meet a being existentially, is the lord of the hour. . . . It steps in between and shuts off from us the light of Heaven.[13]

As a result, modern man's relation to nature has become distant, manipulating, and exploitative. If an ecological ethic is to be developed, nature must be re-

[11] In *The Shaking of the Foundations* (New York: Scribners, 1955), p. 76.

[12] *I and Thou* (New York: Scribners, 1958).

[13] *To Hallow This Life*, ed. Jacob Trapp (New York: Harper, 1958), p. 117.

spected as a Thou. Without It no one can live. But as Buber notes: "He who lives with It alone is not a man."[14]

A Land Ethic

Devastation of land is not a new phenomenon. It began long ago with neolithic man, who used fire to clear forest land for grazing.[15] Succeeding civilizations misused the land; forests disappeared, often leaving deserts. American pioneers moving westward wore out farms until the frontier was pushed into the Pacific. The industrial revolution and modern technology have added to the devastation of nature. In the wake of these movements, forests have been cut and a great deal of rich soil washed away by erosion. Our natural resources have been depleted through overuse by technology. Today green spaces disappear almost overnight, giving way to urban sprawl, air strips, miles of interstate highways, and strip mining. Now all of our wildernesses are threatened by land developers, lumber men, vast farm corporations, and surface mining companies.

An ecological ethic demands new land-use policies embodying a land ethic that will preserve our natural resources and make for a better quality of life. But this will never happen without an ecological conscience.

Ethics and Progress

An ecological ethic will challenge the view of material progress that is current in America. The time is overdue for the nation to ask where it is being carried by what Schweitzer calls a "will-to-progress" that has lost its rootage in moral ideals.[16]

We hear a great deal about the Gross National Prod-

14 *I and Thou,* p. 34.
15 Lamont C. Cole, "Playing Russian Roulette with Biogeochemical Cycles," in *The Environmental Crisis.*
16 *Out of My Life and Thought,* p. 122.

uct (GNP) as the benchmark of prosperity and progress. When it recently reached one trillion dollars, it was celebrated as a milestone in economic history. This is a misleading and false notion of progress. Some students estimate that nearly half of the GNP consists of socially useless and ecologically disastrous products.[17] Stress on the kind of material progress reflected by a high GNP has resulted in a loss of spiritual depth and an overuse of natural resources for immediate, selfish ends.

Kenneth Boulding, the economist, notes that the GNP is too gross to measure even material progress.[18] It includes numerous items that should be netted out: the depreciation of capital, the military and defense industries, commuting, pollution, and products of no real social value. What needs to be done now, says Boulding, is to shift from an open or "cowboy" economy (the cowboy being symbolic of reckless, exploitative, romantic, and violent behavior) to a closed or "spaceman" economy (symbolic of the earth as a spaceship with limited resources in which man must find his place in a cyclical ecological system).[19] The cowboy economy maximizes consumption and production as though natural resources were inexhaustible. The spaceman economy minimizes these factors and sees the real measure of success in the quality of life. To maximize the welfare of this generation and to increase the GNP will short-change future generations, who will inherit problems that should be solved now.

The "will-to-progress" must be geared to the ethical ends of welfare for all creatures and things. It must be

---

17 *Eco-Catastrophe* (New York: Harper, 1970), p. ix.

18 "Fun and Games with the Gross National Product — The Role of Misleading Indicators in Social Policy," in *The Environmental Crisis,* p. 161.

19 "The Economics of the Coming Spaceship Earth," in *The Environmental Handbook,* ed. Garrett DeBell (New York: Ballantine, 1970), p. 96.

pointed in the direction of quality instead of quantity. Hence, progress should be redefined in terms of making human life truly human and keeping it that way. An ecological standard of living must be substituted for the current economic standard. American society, organized around production for profit, will have to develop a planned, ecologically balanced program involving a reordering of priorities and the wise use of natural resources, so as to improve the quality of both life and the environment.

Ethics and Technology

In a penetrating analysis of the moral impact of our technological mentality and computerized culture, Ian Barbour identifies four great dangers of the technological mentality: the exploitation of the environment, reliance on power, impoverishment of experience in terms of man's loss of imagination and emotional life, and unqualified reliance on technology.[20] Barbour is neither a technophobe nor a technophile. Rather he advocates the humanization of the technological revolution. Technology must be redirected so that it will deal effectively with the threats of nuclear war, the population explosion, poverty and hunger in the Third World, and the environmental problem in the industrial West.

Jacques Ellul speaks of a "technological morality," which tends to set up a new scale of values and virtues in terms of technology. This morality exhibits three basic characteristics: (1) it is a morality of behavior, solely interested in man's external behavior; (2) it does not require that man act well, but that he act normally; and (3) it takes success to be a clear sign of virtue.[21] Ellul insists that steps must be taken to move humanity

20 *Science and Secularity: The Ethics of Technology* (New York: Harper, 1970), pp. 61-73.

21 *To Will and To Do* (Philadelphia: Pilgrim, 1969), pp. 185-193.

out of the environment that technology is producing for its own needs.

Barbour is realistic about seeking technological solutions for the environmental problems. Piecemeal approaches that deal only with symptoms are inadequate. If man's basic attitudes are not changed, "man's predatory spirit will only find new ways to plunder the earth."[22] Hence, he suggests a "re-orientation of values and goals, a shift from a 'Thing-oriented society' to a 'person-oriented' and 'life-oriented' culture."[23]

Man has at his disposal the technological knowledge and means to achieve a world in which there can be an optimum population with a decent standard of living for all people. But politics, selfishness, and greed prevent it. Somehow the level of teamwork, cooperation, energy, and technical skill demonstrated in putting man on the moon must be directed toward solving the problems of poverty, inferior education, substandard housing, inequality of opportunity, racism, the deterioration of cities, pollution, and the unchecked growth of population on a global scale.

An Ethic of Human Reproduction

The ecological ethic we have been describing must make provision for responsible human reproduction. Human proliferation is a primary cause of environmental degradation and thus a threat to the quality of life of the inhabitants of the earth. An ethical style of life must be adopted, then, which will result in slowing the rapid population growth. The right to procreate must be limited to the ability of parents adequately to care for their children and the environment.

While there are no scriptural prooftexts to support the Christian in practicing planned parenthood, there

22 *Op. cit.,* p. 7.
23 *Ibid.,* p. 141.

are principles that serve as guidelines. In the first place, the primary purpose of marriage is unitive, not procreative, relational, not reproductive (Gen. 2:24). The injunction "be fruitful and multiply" is from Genesis 1, a later tradition. Nowhere does Jesus, Paul, or any other New Testament writer speak of marriage in terms of the so-called "command" to "fill the earth" (Gen. 1:28), but always in terms of the "one flesh" relationship.

In the second place, love in the biblical sense means to will the welfare of others. Obviously, this applies as well to the matter of procreation and rearing children: parents have a moral obligation to plan for the number of children they can adequately provide for.

Christian parents, in the light of love, evaluate their situation, decide the number of offspring they can care for, and mutually adopt birth control methods they will use to achieve this goal. If the principle of love were honestly followed by all parents, it would result in slowing down the population growth and improve the quality of life in the family and society.

Ecological Asceticism

With only 6 percent of the world's population, the United States consumes 50 percent of the resources and produces 50 percent of the pollution of the earth. Americans seem caught up in an orgy of consumerism. Millions of dollars are spent annually on gadgets that have little or no value for improving the quality of life. As we saw in the preceding chapter, a conscious effort is made to create a demand for more goods, often worthless, and to promote more consumption. According to some scholars, more money is spent on advertising and sales promotion in America — with its doctrines of planned obsolescence and consumer manipulation — than on all education, public and private, elementary through the universities.[24]

Dorothy Sayers has observed that "a society in which consumption has to be artificially stimulated in order to keep production going is a society founded on trash and waste, and such a society is a house built upon sand."[25] In response to this situation, Frederick Elder suggests a new asceticism for Western society.[26] By this he does not mean withdrawing from the world like medieval hermits or monks, but searching for a new way of acting with the world. Restraint, emphasis upon quality of existence, and reverence for life are the basic ingredients of this new style of life. All of this calls for a simpler kind of existence. John Cobb declares that we need "a new ethic of scarcity" and a new self-discipline. This new asceticism, according to Cobb, will

> ... encourage those enjoyments, physical and spiritual, that do not use up our resources or pollute the environment — personal creativity, the arts, sports, education, psychological growth, sensual pleasure, celebration — while rejecting those that do — fine homes, private automobiles, jet planes, disposable containers, unnecessary food and clothing.[27]

This call is echoed by Ralph Nader, who challenges those college students who militantly profess to be escaping the ratrace of their parents:

> The average student spends two hundred and fifty dollars a year for soft drinks and tobacco and movies. If they would contribute only three dollars per student per year, they could recruit the toughest, finest lawyers to begin dealing with pollution and corrup-

[24] *Eco-Catastrophe,* p. ix.
[25] *Creed or Chaos* (New York: Harcourt-Brace, 1949), p. 46.
[26] *Crisis in Eden* (Nashville: Abingdon, 1970), pp. 145f.
[27] "Ecological Disaster and the Church," *The Christian Century,* October 7, 1970, pp. 1186-1187.

tion. . . . Being stoned on marijuana isn't very different from being stoned on gin.[28]

Nader concludes that what we need is "a new Spartan ethic in this country, particularly among the young."[29]

To aid the individual in his quest for ecological asceticism, the rich nations of the world could de-emphasize economic activities that merely multiply the production and consumption of goods and "design a low-consumption economy of stability . . . in which there is much more equitable distribution of wealth than in the present one."[30]

An Ethic of Work

Throughout the history of Protestantism, work has been a most significant — even sanctified — fact of life. Christian calling and the economic virtues of capitalism coalesced, giving work a religious sanction and linking it to an income-producing job. When the middle-class virtues of thrift, honesty, sobriety, temperance, zeal, and frugality coincided with the religious virtues of a disciplined life, they were accorded a sacredness that the Reformers did not intend. Work came to be seen as the duty of every able-bodied person, idleness as a sin. The popular nineteenth-century hymn, "Work for the Night is Coming," reflected this notion of the Christian's duty to work. To secure wealth by hard work became an honorable ambition. Indeed, riches were seen as God's blessings upon the rich man for his labors.[31]

In recent years, the Protestant work ethic has come

[28] Quoted by Sam Blum, "Ralph Nader: The Man Who Makes Waves," *Redbook,* Nov. 1971, p. 76.

[29] *Ibid.*

[30] Paul and Anne Ehrlich, *Population, Resources, Environment: Issues in Human Ecology,* p. 325.

[31] Especially noteworthy among the mass of literature on this subject are Max Weber's *The Protestant Ethic and the Spirit of Capitalism* and R. H. Tawney's *Religion and the Rise of Capitalism.*

under criticism.[32] It is argued that this ethic is unrealistic in the light of advancing technology and increased leisure time. Work must no longer be seen to be synonymous with an income-producing job, but must be redefined and emancipated from the realm of religious duty. Whether a person works or not, says Harvey Cox, he should receive an income simply because he is a human being.[33]

It is the case that man is a worker — often a compulsive one. Many people feel that it is a religious duty to work, and sometimes their work becomes idolatrous. But work need not for that reason be disassociated from the Christian faith. Nor should work, on the other hand, be identified with the Christian doctrine of calling. Every Christian is called to be a minister — that is, to the work of Christ — regardless of his earthly job. His earthly labor is only incidental to his call to be a Christian. His job is a means of implementing his calling as a servant of Christ, if it meets human needs.[34]

Much useless work is done which adds to the problem of consumerism and pollution. Employment must be seen as more than a mere job. Rather a job must be a useful one, which meets real human needs, not an artificial one pressed upon the public by high pressure advertising. More work must be channeled in the direction of the enormous number of things that are being left undone. The herculean task of cleaning up the environment and keeping it clean would absorb the entire unemployment force in this country. The billions of dollars spent on the military, on the war in Southeast Asia, and on an Alice-in-Wonderland foreign aid program could provide work for millions of people in this country. This would certainly be useful work, for it would

32 See, for example, Cameron P. Hall, compiler, *Human Values and Advancing Technology* (New York: Friendship, 1967), p. 125; and Harvey Cox, *The Secular City* (New York: Macmillan, 1965), Chapter 8.
33 *Op. cit.*, p. 191.
34 See my *Has God Called You?* (Nashville: Broadman, 1969).

attack not only the unemployment and poverty problems, but the environmental problem as well.

Besides employment in the ecological enterprise, there
are thousands of service roles in which men and women
can find fulfillment. In the field of education, possibili-
ties for creative work are almost unlimited. To mention but a few, work in the area of health, care of the
aged, the legal profession, and recreation need to be
done on a massive scale. Such work is directly related to
improving the quality of life and to making society a
healthier home for the human spirit.

An Ethic of Alliance

One of the hopeful signs today is the growing openness of scientists, humanists, and theologians to a com-
bined effort to develop an interdisciplinary ethics for
survival. The gap between these groups is being bridged
at the point of ethical concern for the future of man
and his environment. One example is that of biologist
Van R. Potter who proposes a new discipline called
"Bioethics" as a bridge between science and the humani-
ties.[35] He rightly notes that ethical values cannot be
separated from biological facts and ecology. Bioethics
aims at the goals of wisdom and knowledge, wisdom being defined as the knowledge of how to use knowledge
for survival and the social good. Hence, values are tested
in terms of the future. Actions that decrease the chance
of survival are immoral; conversely, those which increase
the chance of survival are right and good.

Christian ethics, in search for a social policy for ecology, may make common cause with the goals of the scientists and humanists. At the same time Christian love
may be informed by the best insights of all value systems.
In so doing Christian ethics will remain distinctive and

---

[35] *Bioethics: Bridge to the Future* (Englewood Cliffs, N.J.: Prentice-
Hall, 1970).

dominant for the Christian. Such an alliance will lend realism to the Christian ethic and relate it concretely to the ecological problem.

Large-scale mobilization of scientists, educators, economists, politicians, and theologians is demanded in order adequately to cope with the ecological problem. Too long each of these groups has "done its own thing" in attacking social evils without relating to the others. The theologian can provide motivation and ethical wisdom, the scientist the necessary facts, the economist a plan for a more just economic system, the politician legislation and implementation, and the educator the dissemination of knowledge. All must join in their efforts to reverse the ecocidal process and to plan for a better quality of life for this and future generations.

Ethical findings must be implemented in terms of concrete action. In the next chapter we shall examine some practical steps toward reducing environmental deterioration and improving the quality of life.

4

Strategies for Survival

Science can reveal the depth of the crisis,
but only social action can resolve it.
> — Barry Commoner

The survival of mankind depends on immediate and global control of the problems of pollution and over-population. ("Survival" is the correct term to use in discussing the environmental issue. Some conservationists and exponents of beautification still talk in terms of aesthetics, but the problems have advanced to a stage where solving them is a matter of avoiding ecological disaster.) The word ecotactics has been coined to describe the use of all available forces against the enemies of the environment.[1] The number of publications explaining how activists can work for a better environment is increasing. (Many of these titles are listed in the bibliography at the end of this book.) In the pages

[1] John Mitchell and Constance Stallings, eds., *Ecotactics* (New York: Pocket Books, 1970), p. 5.

below we offer some concrete suggestions for the ecologically concerned.

Personal Ecotactics

"Do-it-yourself-ecology" is becoming popular. Among
the organizations in which one can participate are the
Sierra Club, Friends of the Earth, Zero Population
Growth, Inc., Planned Parenthood, and hundreds of
other groups that serve as vehicles for ecological action.
(A list of some of these is found on pp. 108-109 below.)

At the individual level, one can avoid purchasing non-
biodegradable containers, nonreturnable bottles, phosphate detergents, and similar items whose disposal contributes to polluting the environment. Joining a car
pool, riding a bicycle, or walking to work will cut down
on auto pollution. One may take the Anti-Litter pledge
to "reconsider before you litter" sponsored by the Isaak
Walton League of America. A more drastic type of radical individual action is that undertaken by a person in
the Chicago area who calls himself "The Fox." The Fox
operates as a sort of anti-pollution "Zorro." One of
his tactics is to walk into the lobby of a company that is
polluting rivers and lakes and dump a bucket of the
disagreeable effluents on the floor.

Pollution bounty hunters have been recruited by Rep-
resentative Henry S. Reuss of Wisconsin, the chairman
of a House Government Operations subcommittee.
Reuss is encouraging his constituents to take advantage
of the 1899 Rivers and Harbours Act, which provides
payment to individuals who catch others dumping foreign substances and pollutants into navigable waters
without a permit from the Army Corps of Engineers.
The bounty is one-half the fine (a maximum of $2500)
for each incident or day of violation. The congressman's
office said over 2500 bounty-hunting kits were mailed
to would-be citizen investigators after Reuss's subcom-

mittee discovered this old law.[2] Two teachers who explored rivers around Pittsburgh in search of pollution provided the data that led to the conviction of a corporation for discharging refuse into the Monongahela River. A U.S. District Court jury found Pennsylvania Industrials Chemical Corporation guilty of four counts of dumping waste into navigable waters. This was the first jury conviction based on information furnished by citizens under the 1899 law.

Personal ecotactics are important, but they must be extended to collective social ecotactics, not allowed to become a substitute for more radical change in the social order.

Recycling

Some pollutants can be converted into things of value through the process known as recycling.[3] Some industries are discovering that there is profit in waste. Hence, glass, waste paper, plastics and other items are now being recycled into new and useful products at a profit. The Louisville *Courier-Journal and Times* for Sunday, Sept. 27, 1970, printed one section on recycled paper from 92,000 old newspapers discarded by households in Jefferson County. This section of recycled paper saved 391 trees from being cut and becoming newsprint. Also it reduced the amount of trash collected daily by the city.

Other uses can be made of waste to reduce the overuse of natural resources. Fossil fuels can be conserved by burning garbage for power. Derelict cars can be recycled into steel. Bottles can be crushed and melted and made into new ones. Research is needed to discover still more ways of recycling all waste and pollution.

[2] *Look,* August 11, 1970; see also the Louisville *Times,* Feb. 6, 1971, p. A-1; June 30, 1971, p. A-15.
[3] "Special Report: Turning Junk and Trash into a Resource," *Business Week,* Oct. 10, 1970, p. 65.

Mass Transportation

The automobile is a major source of pollution. Americans purchase about 35,000 cars every day, and scrap about 25,000. At present there is one car, truck or bus for every two Americans. While they are on the road, autos are a leading cause of air pollution; after they are discarded, they are a leading cause of junk.

Over half the air pollution can be traced to automobiles, which emit about 450 million pounds of carbon monoxide into the air every day. Today every major city has dangerous concentrations of this deadly gas in its air.

The development of adequate rapid mass transportation systems could take millions of cars off city streets, and thus reduce the poisons in the air we breathe. And even if the automakers produce a pollution-free engine, mass transportation will be necessary to relieve traffic and parking problems in cities.

Political Pressure

For all the value in individual ecotactics, political action is necessary if the ecological problem is ever to be solved. Individual and collective pressure must be brought to bear on apathetic politicians, urging them to enact and enforce legislation about ecological issues. The public must prod politicians to pass stiff anti-pollution measures against the big polluters such as industry, the military, and business. Light fines and reprimands are inadequate penalties for polluting the air we breathe, the water we drink, and the food we eat.

To solve the pollution problem in America several environmental policies will have to be established. Senator Gaylord Nelson advocates national policies on land use, elimination of the ghetto, on air and water quality, recycling of wastes, on resource management, of technology assessment, and of citizens' environmental rights.[4] To adopt these policies will be costly to both industry and the taxpayer, but failure to do so will be even more costly in the long run. Efforts to clean up the environment must not be confined to school children periodically picking up trash and to academic rhetoric. Radical changes in our society must take place.

At the international level ways must be discovered to require all nations to abide by international laws to protect the environment in which all people live. It is hoped that the representatives of the United Nations meeting in Stockholm, June 1972, will produce concrete plans for a world program of environmental control.

Ecological Education

The development of an ecological conscience among Americans and other people of the world will require what Ralph Nader calls a massive "fish bowl" disclosure of "the flow of silent violence" affecting their health and safety.[5] Massive exposure of the ecological problem through education at all levels is one of the most effective means of coping with the issue.

No effective ecological action can be taken if the facts of the situation are unknown. The educational system is the instrument by which these facts can be made known on a sustained basis and a massive scale. As Stephanie Mills puts it: "We must hit home, through the educational process, that our environment is not a Davey Crockett-hat fad. We cannot put it on and take it off, because if we take it off we are going to die."[6]

[4] "This Generation's Strategy to Save the Environment," *Agenda for Survival* (New Haven: Yale U.P., 1970), pp. 190-195.

[5] "The Profits of Pollution," *The Progressive,* April 1970, p. 20.

[6] "Action Imperative for Population Control: A Woman's View," *Agenda for Survival,* p. 134.

Population Control

We have mentioned above how rapidly the population of the world is increasing. The reasons for this are numerous, among them advances in medical science, industry, technology, and agriculture. Many theories and programs have been advanced to curb population growth, such as increased food production, foreign aid programs, education, and birth control. The last mentioned is considered by many as the most effective way to deal with burgeoning population.

Various methods of birth control are currently available: the condom, the diaphragm, the cervical cap, a variety of creams and jellies, the rhythm method, the pill, and the intrauterine device (IUD). In the near future new methods will become generally available. A "morning-after" pill is now being developed which can be taken a few days after coitus. A "time capsule" of steroid, to be implanted under the skin, may be effective up to thirty years. These and other methods are still in the experimental stage.

Sterilization is one of the most effective means of birth control. The operation on the male — called vasectomy — is quite simple and results, in almost all cases, in complete sterilization. The operation takes about twenty to thirty minutes and can be performed in the doctor's office. The doctor will require a conference with husband and wife and obtain a signed release exonerating him in case surgery is not effective. Usually the doctor will not do the vasectomy unless the husband is thirty-five years or older and already has two or more children. The cost of a vasectomy in the United States is approximately one hundred dollars; in Britain the operation is free under the provisions of the National Health Service Law. At present the chance that the operation can be reversed is rather small.

The operation for sterilization of the female is called

a salpingectomy. The surgery is more complicated, because it involves an internal surgical operation and
anesthesia. A section of the fallopian tube is removed to
prevent passage of the ova.

Neither vasectomy nor salpingectomy ends the capacity
for sexual performance. Sperm and egg are still manu-
factured by the body, but are not released in an or-
gasm or an ejaculation.

Abortion as a method of birth control is very contro-
versial, because of religious and humanistic views about
the rights of the unborn child. Three basic views on
abortion now prevail in this country. Some people hold
that no abortion should be performed under any cir-
cumstances, because the fetus is a human or a potential
human being. It is argued that the individual's unique
genetic code or genotype is established at the moment
of the fertilization. Hence, the zygote itself — the fer-
tilized egg — should be considered human. Secondly, a
modified approach views abortion as legitimate in case
of rape, incest, danger to the mother's physical and mental health, and in the case of a malformed fetus. A third
view is that of abortion on demand, which holds that
it is an individual matter between a licensed physician
and a female. Advocates of this position argue that no
woman should be forced to have an unwanted child.
To the charge that abortion is murder or feticide, they
counter that no one *knows* whether life begins with the
zygote, the implantation of the zygote in the uterus, or
at birth. By what moral authority, they ask, do we con-
demn an accidental embryo to grow into an unwanted
and unloved child? If one agrees that malformed fetuses
may be aborted, why not also unwanted fetuses, who
will become victims of a malformed spirit and a mu-
tilated psyche?

So the debate goes on. The second view discussed
above appears to be gaining favor among the people in
America. In 1967 Colorado enacted a liberalized abor-

tion law. New York State made abortion legal in 1970 and nearly 165,000 abortions were performed in New York City alone during the first year of the state's legalized law. No doubt other states will adopt various forms of legalized abortion.

Abortion has now become a political issue, a sure sign that a large segment of voters favor it, some, to be sure, for reasons of personal convenience, but others as a means to reverse the population explosion. For the latter group the goal is "zero population" growth (a two-child family as the norm). Bills have been introduced in the Senate to legalize abortion in all fifty states. One bill has been introduced which would authorize abortions performed by licensed physicians upon request by any female within the first twenty weeks of pregnancy. Senator Robert Packwood of Oregon has proposed that free family planning information be made available to all women; that legal restrictions on abortions be eliminated, to permit women to control their own fertility by early termination of pregnancy; and that a government taxation policy be enacted which encourages small families. He notes that tax incentives are used to encourage many enterprises, including oil exploration, and should include the population crisis.[7]

Packwood's approach to the population problem is voluntaristic. However, there is an increasing number of writers who claim that coercion should be used. Paul Ehrlich argues that America uses coercion in waging war and imposing taxes, and he thinks that some compulsory restrictions on reproduction may be justified.[8]

In any event, abortion is a sure method of controlling population growth. In Japan, for example, where birth

[7] "Stop at Two," *Earth Day — The Beginning* (New York: Bantam Books, 1970), pp. 199-200.

[8] See Paul and Anne Ehrlich, *Population, Resources, Environment,* pp. 273-274; Garrett Hardin, "The Tragedy of the Commons," *Science,* Dec. 13, 1968, pp. 1243-1248; and Edgar Chasteen, *The Case for Compulsory Birth Control* (Englewood Cliffs, N. J.: Prentice-Hall, 1971).

control has been a national policy since 1949, there were 20 million legal abortions up to 1964. During this time the birthrate dropped from 34.3 in 1949 to 16.5. About 70 percent of the reduction is attributed to legalized abortions.

Overpopulation is a global problem. Some sort of international program for population control is necessary. Perhaps some effective program could be implemented by the United Nations to join forces with numerous private and semi-private organizations such as the International Planned Parenthood Federation and the Ford and Rockefeller Foundations operating in underdeveloped countries where the population is skyrocketing. Education in family planning, improvement in the economic standard of living, increased food production through advanced agricultural techniques, and better medical care on a worldwide scale are essential to achieving an optimum population and preventing mass starvation now and in the future.

A Livable Environment

All of the above strategies aim at achieving an optimum pollution and population in our environment. Obviously all pollution cannot be eliminated from the earth. Hence, the goal is to achieve a livable environment. Mere survival is not enough. The achievement of an optimum pollution and population is essential to making and keeping human life human. Among the basic human rights at stake are the right to eat well, to breathe clean air, to have decent housing, to enjoy natural beauty, to hunt and to fish, to enjoy silence, to be protected from pesticide poisoning, to be free from thermonuclear war, to educate children, to have grandchildren and great-grandchildren.[9] In practical ways these rights spell out Christian *agape* to fellow human

9 Ehrlich, *The Population Bomb,* pp. 187-188.

beings, including those yet unborn. Unless these rights are recognized, preserved, and promoted by the individual and his institutions, the ecological problem will not be corrected. To fail to act now in massive concert will hasten the day of ecological Armageddon.

5

Toward a Theology for Ecology

> What we do about ecology depends on our ideas of
> the man-nature relationship. More science and more
> technology are not going to get us out of the present
> ecologic crisis until we find a new religion, or re-
> think our old one.
>
> — Lynn White, Jr.

For many years most theologians have neglected to
address themselves to a theology for the environment,
particularly inorganic reality. Paul Tillich was one of
the first to call attention to this lack in contemporary
theology: "The religious significance of the inorganic is
immense, but it is rarely considered by theology. . . . A
'theology of the inorganic' is lacking."[1]

Trends Toward an Eco-Theology

Now that the scientists and the secular media have
made the details of the ecological crisis familiar to all,

[1] *Systematic Theology*, Vol. III (Chicago: U. of Chicago Press, 1963),
p. 18.

a number of theologians have begun trying to relate theology meaningfully to the problem.[2] Some — the process theologians — are drawing on Whiteheadian philosophy as a basis for a theology that sees God as present in nature but not identified with it in a pantheistic sense.[3] Others — the future-oriented theologians — are rehabilitating eschatology in theology. They say little about nature as such, but they do take history seriously, stress hope, envision the unity of the whole world, and see the kingdom of God pressing proleptically from the future into the present with transforming power.[4] Closely related to this theology is a trend toward the recovery of the significance of apocalypticism for doing theology. Apocalyptic theology provides, Carl Braaten declares, "a universal perspective on living relations between man and the natural world."[5] The apocalyptic vision provides a cosmic eschatology:

> The apocalyptists grasped the idea that the whole universe of reality is being drawn through struggle and conflict, and pain into the final unity of God. Not only individual men, not merely mankind as a whole, but the whole creation, including the stars and the planets, the winds and the waves, the rocks and the flowers, the animals and even our bodies, is headed toward total salvation. Nature is not sloughed

[2] Among the few works dealing specifically with environmental theology are Conrad Bonifazi, *A Theology of Things* (Philadelphia: Lippincott, 1967); H. Paul Santmire, *Brother Earth* (New York: Nelson, 1970); Frederick Elder, *Crisis in Eden* (Nashville: Abingdon, 1970); Eric Rust, *Nature: Eden or Desert?* (Waco, Tex.: Word, 1971).

[3] See Daniel D. Williams, *The Forms and Spirit of Love* (New York: Harper, 1968); John Cobb, Jr., *A Christian Natural Theology* (Philadelphia: Westminster, 1965); Schubert Ogden, *The Reality of God* (New York: Harper, 1966); and Norman Pittenger, *Process Thought and Christian Faith* (New York: Macmillan, 1968).

[4] Jürgen Moltmann, *The Theology of Hope* (New York: Harper, 1967); Wolfhart Pannenberg, *Jesus, God and Man.*

[5] "The Significance of Apocalypticism for Systematic Theology," *Interpretation*, p. 496. See also Allan Galloway, *The Cosmic Christ* (New York: Harper, 1951).

off so that souls can soar freely into an ethereal state of weightlessness.[6]

With the revival of interest in the apocalyptic vision of the Bible, an ecological theology is now more possible. Ecologically minded theologians will welcome this new concern because apocalypticism includes a respect for nature, sets forth the concept of the ultimate unity of all things in God, and emphasizes the vision of "a new heaven and a new earth."

Valuable insights for an ecological theology will come from other disciplines. From the philosophical perspective, relevant clues can be found in the works of Alfred North Whitehead and Charles Hartshorne.[7] Scientists are also making significant contributions toward a theistic approach to the universe. Charles Birch and other scientists have a vision of God within the natural process.[8] Writers in a variety of fields are becoming aware that the ecological issue is at its roots religious and cannot be solved without a radical religious outlook. Paul Goodman, educator and novelist, believes that "a kind of religious transformation" analogous to the Protestant Reformation is necessary to meet the environmental problem.[9] The economist Kenneth Boulding advocates a dialogue with Eastern religions to learn how to live in harmony with nature.[10] Howard T. Odum, ecologist, suggests that the natural sector be included in our religious system. He challenges the churches and church-related institutions to open their doors to this

6 *Op. cit.,* p. 497.

7 Especially Whitehead, *Process and Reality* (London: Cambridge U. P., 1924); *Religion in the Making* (Cleveland: World, 1961); Charles Hartshorne, *The Divine Relativity* (New Haven: Yale U. P., 1964).

8 *Nature and God* (Philadelphia: Westminster, 1965).

9 "Can Technology Be Human?" *Ecological Conscience: Values for Survival,* ed. Robert Disch (Englewood Cliffs, N. J.: Prentice-Hall, 1970), pp. 116-117.

10 "The Wisdom of Man and the Wisdom of God," *Human Values on the Spaceship Earth* (New York: National Council of Churches, 1966), p. 14.

new religion with the hope that a "new and more powerful morality may emerge through the dedication of the millions of men who have faith in the new networks and endeavor zealously for them."[11]

We quoted Lynn White at the head of this chapter as saying that we are not going to deal effectively with the eco-crisis "until we find a new religion, or rethink our old one."[12] I believe the "old religion" — the Judeo-Christian faith — needs to be rethought along several lines: an examination of the biblical doctrines of God, man, and nature, with the view to discovering their relevance to the current environmental crisis.

It may be objected that the ecological issue is too immediately critical for us to take the time for leisurely theological reflection. Instead, we must forge some kind of ecological ethic. But what people do to, for, and with others and their environment depends largely upon what they think of God, nature, themselves, and their destiny. Man's behavior is basically determined by his religious convictions or ultimate concerns. Thus, the only proper way to proceed is to develop a theology and ethic of environmental responsibility simultaneously.

The Creator

In a sublime sentence the prophet declares: "The Lord is the everlasting God, the Creator of the ends of the earth" (Isa. 40:26). As Creator, God is the source of all creatures and things — organic and inorganic — in the universe. "In the beginning God created the heavens and the earth" (Gen. 1:1) by his word and spirit, which brought order out of chaos. All things were made by him and without him what exists would not exist (John 1:1-3). In bringing order out of chaos, God gave order

[11] *Environment, Power, and Society* (New York: Wiley, 1971), pp. 249, 310.

[12] "The Historical Roots of Our Ecologic Crisis," *Science,* 155:1203, 1967.

and harmony to his creation and we understand this fact by faith (Heb. 11:13; cf. II Pet. 3:5).

That God is creator of the universe is the basic tenet of the Christian faith. The first article of the Apostles' Creed states: "I believe in God the Father Almighty, Maker of heaven and earth." This doctrine is the ground, Langdon Gilkey declares, "in which the other beliefs of the Christian faith are based. It affirms what the Christian believes about the status of God in the whole realm of reality: He is the Creator of everything else."[13] By divine revelation we learn *who* made and sustains the universe and all things therein. This conviction is basic to any effort at solving the ecological crisis. As T. S. Eliot has observed, "a wrong attitude towards nature implies, somewhere, a wrong attitude towards God, and the consequence is an inevitable doom."[14]

Little is revealed in the Genesis accounts about the method God employed in creation or how long ago this took place. The traditional view that God created the world in six literal days in 4004 B.C., as worked out by Archbishop Ussher, is no longer tenable. Since the middle of the nineteenth century, theologians have generally accepted the view that God employed evolution as an instrument in creating the universe over a period of billions of years. To the extent that the scientific theory of evolution does not pretend to explain the ultimate causation of the universe, it does not contradict the biblical view of creation. Rather it supplements it.

Many conservative theologians now admit that the universe emerged before 4000 B.C. Some read the words of II Peter 3:8 — "But do not ignore this one fact, beloved, that with the Lord one day is as a thousand years, and a thousand years as one day" — to allow for a creation period of six thousand years, a thousand years for

13 *Maker of Heaven and Earth* (New York: Doubleday, 1959), p. 15.

14 Quoted by Dorothy Sayers, in *Creed or Chaos* (New York: Harcourt-Brace, 1949), p. 41.

each of the six days of creation referred to in Genesis. But Genesis is a religious interpretation, not a scientific document describing how the world began. Failing to recognize this, literalists distort the meaning of the Genesis account and contribute thus to a polarization in the theological and scientific communities, not to mention a credibility gap among the educated laity. The literary form of the Genesis account of creation is poetic narrative, which came later in the history of Israel. The Priestly document deliberately excludes mythological motifs.[15] There is no hint in it of such motifs as a conflict in heaven or a struggle among cosmic powers, as are found in Psalm 74 or Psalm 85:9-10 or Isaiah 27:1.

Perhaps the writers of Genesis believed that God did create the world in six 24-hour days. Although this conflicts with the modern scientific view, we should remember that those writers lived in a prescientific era. The crucial article of faith — that God is creator and sustainer of the universe — cannot be challenged by scientific theory nor established by scientific investigation.

The ultimate truth behind the Genesis narratives is that God is the creator and sustainer of the universe, which is utterly dependent upon him for existence. If his sustaining spirit were withdrawn for a moment, all creation would revert to chaos (Job 34:14-15; Ps. 104:29-30). In philosophical terms, "the world lives by its incarnation of God in itself."[16] Through Christ God upholds "the universe by his word of power" (Heb. 1:3). In Christ all things "cohere," that is, they are held together for God's ultimate purpose of cosmic redemption (Col. 1:17).

Thus the power by which God sustains the universe is his own creative power. God adds himself as a force

[15] Brevard Childs, *Myth and Reality in the Old Testament* (*Studies in Old Testament Theology,* No. 27) (London: SCM, 1960), pp. 30-42.
[16] Whitehead, *Religion in the Making,* p. 149.

to the ground of all being from which all creative acts occur. Yet God transcends all temporality; for he is not a derivative from the world, but the source from which the reality of the world is derived.[17] Hence, God is immanent in his creation — not in the pantheistic sense of being identified or totally immersed in it, but in the sense of being *involved* as Creator Spirit and sustainer of the universe.

God cares for and rejoices in his creation. He feeds the birds (Matt. 6:26) and allows no sparrow to fall to the ground without noticing (Matt. 10:29-30; Luke 12:6). He clothes the lilies of the field (Matt. 6:30) and hears the cry of the animals for food (Ps. 104:21-22). He sports with the Leviathan of the sea (Ps. 104:26) and calls every star by name (Ps. 147:4). God rejoices in all that he has created and will create (Isa. 65:17-19). Scripture makes it clear that, while God created all things for man's welfare, they are also a source of the enjoyment and glory of God.

The God of biblical revelation, then, is not a static, but an active being, not an impersonal, but personal reality. He is not the god of the Deists, who supposedly made the universe like a clock, wound it, and then withdrew to let it be governed mechanically by law. Nor is he the god of the pantheist, who is identified and equated with the world. Nor is God the impersonal deity of the philosophers. No, the God of divine revelation is the living, personal God who loves and cares for his creation, involving himself in it without losing his own sovereign integrity or destroying man's freedom and responsibility. His sovereign being of love is constant, transcendent, and unchanged. In the creative acts of his spirit, God involves himself in his creation, suffering with his suffering creatures, and achieving his eternal purpose of redemption in history. The creator God is most fully revealed in his Son, the cosmic Christ, through

17 *Ibid.,* p. 150.

whom and for whom all things were made (Col. 1:15f.) and by whose word of power the universe is being upheld (Heb. 1:1-4).

Creation as God's Realm of Cosmic Redemption

Throughout the centuries many elements in the church have developed a contempt for the natural. This attitude is expressed, for example, in the hymnology of the church. "For the Beauty of the Earth" is one of the few hymns to express praise for God's earth. Far more common is the other-worldly orientation typified by the chorus, "This world is not my home; I'm just a-passing through." Yet in the Psalms, the hymnal of the Hebrews, praise of nature is a central theme.

The traditional view of nature has been that it is a mere stage on which the drama of redemption takes place. As a result, its significance is obscured and it is reduced to mere "scenery" in God's plan of redemption.[18] Nature is not seen as having any intrinsic value or permanent place in the eternal purpose of God.

Now, in the light of the ecological problem, the biblical doctrine of nature must be recovered. This earth must be viewed as something more than a mere stage setting in God's plan for the ages; it must be seen from a biblical perspective as an integral part of God's divine drama of redemption of both man and nature. This will involve a reassessing of traditional theology and widening its scope to include the cosmic dimension of salvation.

Essential to a theology of ecology is the fact of the sacramental quality of nature. The Priestly document

[18] See Karl Barth, *Church Dogmatics*, III, ii, 19, where the chief focus is upon man; and Emil Brunner, *Revelation and Reason*, p. 33, where he refers to the cosmic element in the Bible as "never anything more than 'scenery' in which the history of mankind takes place." Even in his *Ordnungstheologie* in *Das Gebot und die Ordnungen*, published in 1932, the "orders," says Wingren, "have been tacked on"; *op. cit.*, p. 34.

of creation (Gen. 1-2:4) makes plain God's divine satisfaction in all that he has created.[19] God declares that it is "good," "very good" (Gen. 1:10, 12, 18, 21, 31). In contrast to Gnosticism, biblical revelation clearly indicates that nature is not inherently evil, and that God and nature are not antagonistic to each other.

Nature did not fall in the "fall of Adam," though man and nature are so bound up with each other that the natural world is affected by man's sin (Gen. 3:17; Isa. 24:5-6; Jer. 4:17-26). When man sins, nature suffers; when man obeys God, nature sings and rejoices (Jer. 51:48; Isa. 44:22-23). Though the land was cursed in the fall, it did not become sinful and evil. Only man can sin, because he alone has freedom to obey or to disobey God. Man's sin caused a "curse" to fall upon all creation. Nature was subjected to "futility" not because of its own will but because God subjected it (Rom. 8:20). The "principalities and powers" (agents of divine judgment) became embodied in nature as well as social structures. The whole creation now suffers as a result of man's sin and longs for redemption (Rom. 8:19-23).

The incarnation of God in the flesh is further evidence of the goodness of the material. In Jesus, the Word became transparent, so that he could say: "He who has seen me, has seen the Father" (John 14:9). Even in the resurrection, Christ's body was not merely the form, but the substance of a body that could be touched. In the incarnation, God entered all created reality, even nature. As William Temple asserts, "the world, which is the self-expressive utterance of the Divine Word, becomes itself a true revelation, in which what comes is not truth concerning God, but God Himself."[20]

The incarnation of Christ is the final answer to the Gnostic heresy that the "flesh" is evil. But there is no biblical warrant for supposing that the flesh is evil. In

[19] S. R. Driver, *The Book of Genesis* (London: Methuen, 1904), p. 5.
[20] *Nature, Man and God* (London: Macmillan, 1951), p. 493.

the Old Testament, flesh refers to all creatures and in particular to their dependence on God, but carries no sense of moral disparagement or sin (see Gen. 7:21; Job 34:15; Isa. 40:6-8; Joel 2:28). Evil arises not out of the flesh as flesh, but out of an evil impulse that is not in man's physical constitution at all. It stems from his misuse of his free will.

Nor does the New Testament suggest that the flesh has any moral defect. Sin in man does infect his body (II Cor. 7:1; Eph. 2:3), but this does not make the body evil. Paul's view of the body is not that of the Greeks. He anticipated its resurrection (Rom. 8:23) and conceived it to be the temple of the spirit (I Cor. 6:19; cf. Rom. 12:1f.). He does not identify "flesh" (*sarx*) with the body (*soma*). By *sarx*, Paul does not mean the material of which the body consists, but the whole lower nature of man. *Sarx* is a moral category identified with the lower instincts or natural impulses, which are not sinful in themselves, but may become the occasion of sin unless they are mastered. The flesh, then, is not the source of sin, but the "seat of sin." A prooftext often used to identify the flesh as evil is Romans 8:3: "For God has done what the law, weakened by the flesh, could not do: sending his own son in the likeness of sinful flesh and for sin, he condemned sin in the flesh, in order that the just requirement of the law might be fulfilled in us, who walk not according to the flesh but according to the Spirit." Note that Jesus came not "in sinful flesh," but in the "likeness" of sinful flesh. His was real flesh, like our sinful flesh in that it was liable to human needs and infirmities, which are not sinful in themselves but are to us occasions for sinning. The "likeness of sinful flesh" is intended to deny sinfulness, for Christ was sinless (I Pet. 2:22). It was through his flesh that Christ opened a "new and living way" for man (Heb. 10:20).

Spiritual realities are known to man sacramentally

through material or corporeal realities. The bread and the wine of the Lord's Supper (material substances) become the media through which God's spiritual blessings are communicated to man. Hence, the celebration of the Eucharist implies that matter is sacred, as does the resurrection of the body.

Since Christ came in the flesh, the human body and the whole material universe can no longer be viewed — as the Gnostics did — as evil. For this reason man must act responsibly toward his environment, for there is a holiness in nature. Since the material world is an expression of the incarnation of God's power and purpose, man's abuse of it is a sin. To put it more concretely, any "exploitation of man or of matter for commercial uses stands condemned, together with all debasement of the acts and perversions of the intellect."[21]

The New Jerusalem seen in the eschatological perspective of John of the Apocalypse has no temple. This implies the disappearance of the categories of sacred and secular. As Paul Tillich observes regarding the absence of a temple in the new creation, "There will be no secular realm, and for this very reason there will be no religious realm."[22]

An ecological theology will take into account God's covenant relationship to the good universe that he created. His covenant with his people extends to the land (Lev. 25:1-7), as is implicit in the injunction to leave the ground fallow in the seventh year for conservation purposes (Exod. 23:10-11; Lev. 19:9). When Israel's covenant with God was broken, the land suffered. Isaiah declared:

> The earth lies polluted under its inhabitants; for they have transgressed the laws, violated the statutes, broken the everlasting covenant. Therefore a curse devours the earth, and its inhabitants suffer from

21 Sayers, *op. cit.*, p. 42.
22 *The Theology of Culture* (New York: Oxford U. P., 1959), p. 8.

their guilt; therefore the inhabitants of the earth are scorched, and few men are left (Isa. 24:4-6).

To mistreat the land is to break covenant with God and may cause him to "withdraw his presence and providence."[23] When man fails to subdue the earth for God's purpose, it strikes back. The chaos from which God called man begins to return and the land becomes desolate (Ps. 107:33f.; Jer. 49:20; Zeph. 2:9; Job 38:26-29).

God's covenant with nature includes every living creature (Gen. 9:8-17). Trees have their own rights, which are to be respected by man (Deut. 20:19-20). Animals are to be treated with kindness (Exod. 23:4-5; Deut. 22:1-4). Domestic animals are thought to have a covenant with man, whereas wild ones do not and can roam free (Job 41:4). The mother bird is not to be caught when nesting or with young (Deut. 22:6-7).

God's covenant extends to the inorganic (the land, the sun, moon, and stars), for they submit to his creature rule (Ps. 148). Is it not possible that the electrons may "experience" God as they respond to his sustaining energy? Charles Hartshorne asks: "What scientist as such stands up to be counted on the question, where is the lower limit of feeling in the plant-animal series, or [is] even willing to say there is or can be a lower limit?"[24] Of course, the idea that natural entities possess some sort of psychic character (panpsychism) has not been scientifically proved. But there are scientists and philosophers who believe in a form of panpsychism. Charles Birch, a biologist at the University of Sydney, holds that the universe is not "bits of stuff, but that it has, in its ultimate nature, a physical and a mental aspect, never separate but ever conjoined."[25]

Building on Whiteheadian process philosophy, Charles

[23] T. H. Caster, "Earth," in *Interpreter's Dictionary of the Bible,* II, 3.
[24] "Whitehead and Contemporary Philosophy," in *The Relevance of Whitehead,* ed. Ivor Leclerc (New York: Macmillan, 1961), p. 29.
[25] *Nature and God* (Philadelphia: Westminster, 1965), pp. 67-68.

Hartshorne seeks to show God's relationship to his creation in terms of panpsychism. Like Whitehead, Hartshorne espouses a cell theory of "compound individuals." Macroscopic entities are seen as aggregates of sentient occasions of experience. Rocks, for example, are not sentient, but the simplest physical entities of which they are composed are sentient. Their level of sentience may be much lower than that of higher animals, but "this does not preclude their having some degree of feeling, willing, and mentality."[26]

Few theologians would agree with the panpsychism theory, but there are some implications in the Old Testament that nature is capable of psychic response to God and man. Johannes Pederson, eminent Old Testament scholar, notes that the property of a family "belongs to the psychic totality of the family and cannot be divided from it." All that a man possesses and that belongs to his sphere, Pederson claims, is "penetrated by his soul," including his body, tools, house, animals and the "whole of his property."[27]

Some of the biblical writers appear to presuppose some kind of panpsychism in calling upon nature to praise and worship God (Job 38:7; Pss. 89:5; 96:9; Isa. 43:20; 66:23). The land is portrayed as crying out when its owner is unjust:

> If my land has cried out against me, and its furrows have wept together; if I have eaten its yield without payment, and caused the death of its owners; let thorns grow instead of wheat, and foul weeds instead of barley (Job 31:38-40).

Whether this is panpsychism or merely a poetic way of expressing the relation of God and man to nature, it is

[26] *Process Philosophy and Christian Thought,* ed. Delvin Brown, Ralph James, Jr., and Gene Reaves (Indianapolis: Bobbs-Merrill, 1971), p. 29.

[27] *Israel* (London: Oxford U. P., 1926), Vols. I-II, pp. 458-459.

certain that every creature is appointed a place in nature to serve, praise, and glorify God.[28]

A theology for ecology will look at creation as unfinished and in continuous process toward an ultimate goal. "In beginning" (the article "the" is absent), God was creating the universe. That is to say, relatively — not absolutely — at the beginning of the order of things that man observes, God's divine action was creating (cutting to shape) the heavens and the earth, bringing order out of chaos. The Hebrew verb always used for God's creative acts refers to his continuous divine activity in reducing chaos to order. Though God rested from his creative work on the seventh day, he went back to the task the next day. Jesus said: "My Father is working still, and I am working" (John 5:17). The universe is unfinished in the sense that God is shaping it for its final goal: "a new heaven and a new earth" in which he will rule in total righteousness (Isa. 65:17; 66:22; II Pet. 3:13; Rev. 21:1). In the new creation nature "will be set free from its bondage to decay and obtain the glorious liberty of the children of God" (Rom. 8:20-22).

Our language and concepts are of course inadequate to describe the new creation. Teilhard de Chardin speaks of the universe as progressing toward an *omega*-point, a state in which Christ and his faithful followers will leave the world behind and dwell in brotherly love. Santmire challenges this view, correctly I think, as unbiblical because it does not include the redemption of nature. He suggests that it would be more adequate to adopt the idea of an *omega*-world as the telos of the universe.[29] I prefer to use the model of the *omega*-kingdom to designate the telos of the universe. The Revelation of John says that the "kingdom of the world will become the kingdom of God and his Christ who will reign for ever

28 Bernard Anderson, "The Earth is the Lord's: An Essay on the Biblical Doctrine of Creation," *Interpretation,* Jan. 1955, p. 14.

29 *Brother Earth,* p. 108.

and ever" (Rev. 11:15). The *omega*-kingdom will include God's absolute, sovereign, and creative rule over redeemed man, transformed nature, and social structures. Then God's eternal purpose will be achieved: the unification of *all things* in Christ (Eph. 1:10).

Scientific and biblical eschatology have some similar features, but ultimately the two are radically different. Generally scientists hold to the model of an expanding universe that began in an explosion about fifteen billion years ago.[30] How will it all end? No one really knows. According to the Second Law of Thermodynamics, all organized systems of energy will eventually degrade into disorder. The theory of the evolution of dust into living bodies, supported by nuclear theories and experiments, maintains that the sun in our solar system will explode. Each star will become a cinder and every planet revolving around a star will become a burning fireball. When both stars and planets burn out, they will become cold wastelands. Primeval chaos will return. No life will survive this cosmic catastrophe.

Biblical eschatology speaks of "the day of the Lord," when Christ will appear at an unexpected hour (Matt. 24:43-44; Luke 12:39-40; I Thess. 5:2; II Pet. 3:10; Rev. 3:3; 16:15). He will come with judgment of fire. The heavens will pass away with a great noise and the earth shall be burned up (Matt. 24:35; Mark 13:31; Rom. 8:12; II Thess. 1:8; Heb. 1:11; II Pet. 3:10; Rev. 20:11; 21:1). The Old Testament writers share this view:

> Lift up your eyes to the heavens, and look upon the earth beneath: for the heavens shall vanish away like smoke, and the earth shall wax old like a garment (Isa. 51:6; see also Ps. 102:25-26; Isa. 34:4; 65:17; 66:22).

In one respect, the biblical and scientific views of the

30 For a fuller explanation of this theory, see George Gamow, *The Creation of the Universe* (New York: Viking, 1959).

eschaton are similar: the planet earth will be consumed with fire. In the scientific view there is no hope for the cosmos; it will be left void and cold. In the biblical perspective there is a future hope for nature and God's people in a radically transformed world, a new heaven and a new earth.

Just how the cosmos will be transformed into the "new heaven and the new earth" biblical revelation does not say. That remains a mystery known to God alone. The Bible does declare that this present world is "stored up for fire" (II Pet. 3:7), and that a consuming fire is associated with the coming of Christ at the end of the age (Ps. 50:3; Isa. 66:15-16; Dan. 7:10-11; II Pet. 3:10f.). The term "fire" is used symbolically to describe a kind of transformation of the world through judgment and grace. Peter reminds his readers of three worlds: the "old world" destroyed by the flood (II Pet. 3:4), the existing world (v. 7), and the "new world" (v. 13). Just as the flood did not mean the end of the "old world," but a new beginning, the "fire next time" will purify and transform it into a new creation. In the light of the coming crisis, Peter urges his readers to live lives characterized by godliness and holiness, for these virtues will abide when the world is on fire.

Hence, the new and coming creation will be a renewal of the present cosmos. The form, but not the substance, of the first creation will pass away. The old will be fulfilled in the new. All things in heaven and on earth will ultimately find their unity in God, whose purpose it is to unite all things in Christ (Eph. 1:10). The present world, therefore, is a parable of and a prelude to the new.

The whole process of cosmic redemption begins with the personal encounter with Christ as lord of life. As Allan Galloway rightly observes: "It is in this personal encounter with Christ that the doctrine of cosmic redemption must have its foundation if it is to have any foundation at all."[31] It follows, then, that the church, composed of redeemed individuals, becomes the first corporate unit in cosmic salvation. Morever, it is the mission of the church to participate with Christ in breaking down the dividing "walls of hostility" that separate men from God and from each other (Eph. 3:9-10). God's aim of the ages is the production of "one new humanity" of all races. The initial step was taken by the sacrifice of Christ on the cross and the removal of all man-made laws and ordinances that separate races and classes of people (Eph. 2:13-15).

Concerning life in the new creation, the Bible provides only a few hints. In that day there will be no more wars (Isa. 2:4); harmony will prevail between man and animal, and among the animals themselves (Isa. 11:6-9). This "peaceful kingdom" comes about by the reconciliation of all creation to God (Isa. 11:9). Animal life and plant life will be restored to their "unfallen" status in Paradise because of the restoration of the "knowledge of the Lord" (Ezek. 34:25-27; cf. Isa. 35; Joel 3:18; Hos. 2:18-23).

In the new creation, God declares that he will make all things new (Rev. 21:5). There will be no more "sacred" or "secular" distinctions, for there will be no temple: God himself will be the temple. There will be no need for the light of the sun and the moon, for the glory of God will lighten the city (Rev. 21:22-23). God will dwell with his people and there will be no more sorrow, death, crying and pain (Rev. 21:3-4).

The Biblical Model of Man

An ecological theology will also call for a reappraisal of biblical anthropology. The traditional view that man is given a mandate to subdue, dominate, and exploit nature for his own selfish ends must be shown for what

31 *The Cosmic Christ* (New York: Harper, 1951), p. 236.

it is — an unbiblical sanction for raping the earth. The crucial text for this view is Genesis 1:28:

> Be fruitful and multiply, and fill the earth and sub-due it; and have dominion over the fish of the sea and over the birds of the air and over every living thing that moves upon the earth.

This passage has been cited by some writers, as noted in Chapter Two, as the source from which Jews and Christians derive the concept of an anthropocentric universe and legitimation for despoiling the earth.[32] Whatever truth there may be to this charge, to make Genesis 1:28 the root of the current environmental problem is preposterous. Unfortunately, this simplistic explanation has received wide acceptance in academic circles and the press. To hold that Genesis 1:28 provides a blank check for man ruthlessly to exploit nature is bad hermeneutics. When man is viewed from the perspective of the total teaching of the Bible, one gets a radically different view of him and his relation to nature.

The injunction to be fruitful and multiply and fill the earth was necessary in the beginning for the survival of mankind. Today man has filled the earth to the point that overpopulation threatens the support of life: the injunction has largely been fulfilled. Thus, Genesis 1:28 cannot be taken to mean that contemporary man must reproduce to the point of threatening his very existence. Morever, to subdue and to have dominion over all the earth cannot mean that man has the right to destroy it for his own selfish ends.

The eminent Old Testament scholar Gerhard von Rad understands "dominion" as a consequence of being made in the image of God. It was in this context, he

[32] See especially Ian McHarg, "The Plight," in *The Environmental Crisis*, ed. Harold W. Helfrich, Jr., p. 25; and Lynn White, Jr., "The Historical Roots of the Ecologic Crisis," *Science*, Mar. 10, 1967, pp. 1205f.

argues, that man was given dominion over all things.[33] Made in the *imago Dei,* man possesses both dignity and dominion, by which he shares in the sovereignty of God in relation to the world. But man in his pride and selfishness desires to be wholly sovereign and tends to ignore the fact that his dominion is under and limited by the dominion of God. Man is like his creator in that he is free, but there is no dominion without serving God.[34]

When man fails to recognize that his dominion is under the dominion of God, disastrous results follow. Moule puts it succinctly:

> Man is placed in the world by God to be its lord. He is meant to have dominion over it and to use it ... but only for God's sake, only Adam in paradise, cultivating it for the Lord. As soon as he begins to use it selfishly, and reaches out to take fruit which is forbidden by the Lord, instantly the ecological balance is upset and nature begins to groan.[35]

Only when the Priestly document (Gen. 1:1-2:4a) is supplemented by the older Yahwistic narrative of creation (Gen. 2:4b-25) does the full concept of the biblical view of man appear. In the Yahwistic narrative, God places man in the garden to "dress it and to keep it." "Keeping" the garden means, as von Rad rightly observes, "to work in it and preserve it from all damage."[36] Hence, man is placed in the garden not for mere sensual pleasure, but for responsible service, "to prove himself in a realm that was not his own possession."[37]

---

33 *Genesis: A Commentary,* trans. John Marks (London: SCM, 1963), p. 56.

34 Dietrich Bonhoeffer, *Creation and Fall* (New York: Macmillan, 1959), pp. 39-40.

35 *Man and Nature in the New Testament* (Philadelphia: Fortress, 1964), p. 14.

36 *Op. cit.,* p. 78.

37 *Ibid.*

Man, therefore, is a steward or custodian, and not the owner of the earth.

The biblical view of man is that of a "keeper," caretaker, custodian, curator of the *oikos,* the household earth. Man is God's deputy to oversee, direct, and care for the environment. "Steward" is the New Testament term for this role of man in relation to the natural order. It refers to the manager or administrator of an estate. The first requirement of a steward is faithfulness, because he handles that which belongs to another.

Originally the term steward in Anglo-Saxon meant "manager of a sty," that is, a pig pen. After the Prodigal Son had wasted his inheritance, he was forced to become a manager of a sty. If the modern prodigal — the wasteful, polluting spoiler of the earth — continues to force nature to glorify himself instead of the Father in heaven, he may well find himself managing an environmental pig sty, and the original meaning of the term steward will be an ironically accurate description of his situation.

6

The Church and the Ecological Crisis

For the creation waits with eager longing for the revealing of the sons of God.

— St. Paul

The environmental crisis, we have seen, is, to an important extent, a religious and moral one. The church, therefore, has a vital role to play in achieving an optimum environment and the survival of man on this planet. Paul Sears declares that, after several decades of studying the environment and man, he has become certain that "hope lies not in devices but in design, not in technique but in the realm of intangibles — the values and sanctions of our culture. If ever the custodians of religious faith have been challenged, they are challenged today."[1] Ecologists Paul and Anne Ehrlich likewise believe that established religious institutions provide the most effective means of bringing the proper changes in man's outlook on life and the heightening of

[1] "The Injured Earth," in *This Little Planet*, ed. Michael Hamilton (New York: Scribners, 1970), p. 42.

82

society's overall sensitivity to environmental concerns.[2] Ironically, while many Christians in this country are rejecting the institutional church as a means of social change, some scientists are now saying that it is one of our last best hopes of survival.

The Theological Agenda

To become an effective force in environmental renewal, the church must place at the top of her agenda the task of developing a pertinent, relevant theological ethic. Theology is not a set of ossified dogmas, but the servant of revelation by which the truth of God is made meaningful to modern personal and social issues. Theology must be dynamic, freeing itself from rigid, outworn creeds and speaking in new ways to new issues. Whitehead puts it graphically:

> A system of dogmas may be the ark within which the Church floats safely down the flood-tide of history. But the Church will perish unless it opens its windows and lets out the dove to search for an olive branch. Sometimes it will even do well to disembark on Mount Ararat, and build a New Altar to the Divine Spirit — an altar neither in Mount Gerizim nor yet at Jerusalem.[3]

In the face of the ecological crisis the church must redefine its theology to embrace a sacramental view of the universe and to see love in terms of willing the welfare of all God's creatures and things. Christian anthropology must come to an understanding of stewardship that transcends giving a tithe faithfully and sees a responsibility to the whole earth. Men must be seen as co-tenants and stewards of the earth with God and all his creatures.

[2] In *Population, Resources, Environment,* p. 262.
[3] *Religion in the Making* (Cleveland: World, 1961), p. 140.

Inculcating an Ecological Conscience

Robert Disch thinks that if man is to survive the present crisis, he will do so "by developing an ecological psyche, one that will allow him to bridge the gap between his illusions of separateness from and superiority over what he has come to think of as 'nature,' and to recognize that he not only is tied to nature, but that he is nature."[4] Here is where the church can play a significant role: the development of an ecological conscience.

Any church can provide an educational program for every age group to provide facts about the environmental issue and to motivate action toward solving it. Through religious literature, the churches can present the problem to millions of people from the Christian perspective. In the crusade for a better environment, it is precisely that theological dimension of the problem that is being neglected. It is encouraging to observe that churches are now beginning to provide a measure of leadership in this area. Ecological literature, filmstrips, and movies are now available from some denominational headquarters and religious social service commissions.

Study groups, seminars, and dialogues can be formed in churches to study the ecological problem in greater depth. For example, one church provided a week-long concilium on the environment under the title, "Toward an Ecological Conscience." Appropriately the pastor led off with a sermon on the "Theology of Ecology." Experts were recruited to explore with the participants the problems of pollution and overpopulation in the community.

Drama can be an effective means of inculcating this ecological conscience. Talented young people in the church delight in producing and presenting dramas. Eco-dramas may be secured from both religious and

[4] *The Ecological Conscience* (Englewood Cliffs, N. J.: Prentice-Hall, 1971), p. 17.

secular publishers. But both young people and congregation will receive great satisfaction from a home-grown drama that treats the problem of ecology in their own community.

A church camp provides an ideal means of making constituents aware of the environmental problems. Here participants are close to nature and more fully appreciate the need to conserve its beauty. The theme of the encampment could be "Man's Care of God's Earth." Study and recreation during this time would aim at making the participants ecologically conscious and inspiring them to become actively involved with environmental concerns in their homes and communities.

Theological seminaries must orient their curricula more toward ecological concerns. There should be a conscious effort to provide a biblical perspective on the relation of man to nature, to establish interdisciplinary studies that will bridge the gap between theological, sociological, and scientific disciplines; and to help ministers understand the current ecological problem and to suggest concrete ways for motivating active congregational involvement in saving the earth as well as souls.

Occasionally theologians should participate in scientific congresses and conferences, for scientists as well as theologians are interested in the welfare of the world. If the theologian does not pretend to know everything he will usually be well received by scientists. Typical of the openness of scientists to members of the clergy and the church is that of Dr. Howard T. Odum of the Environmental Engineering Department of the University of Florida. He declares:

> We may encourage faster religious change even now by injecting large doses of systems science into the training of religious leaders. What a glorious flood of new revelation of truth God (the essence of the network) has handed man in the twentieth century through sciences and other creative endeavors. How

false are the prophets who refuse even to read about them and interpret the message to the flock. Why do some inhabitants of the church pulpits fight the new revelations simply because the temporary prophets are a million spiritually humble little people in laboratories and libraries, only vaguely aware of their role? Why not open the church doors to the new religion and use the preadopted cathedrals and best ethics of the old to include the new?[5]

The clergyman's role in developing an ecological conscience in the congregation is very important. His primary task is to proclaim the gospel of creation, redemption, and stewardship. For the redemption of man and nature are inseparable. The whole gospel includes the whole world. Hence, the minister will stress the redemption of the natural world as well as the salvation of man who inhabits it.

Texts for preaching on environmental deterioration may easily be found in the Bible. Among these are the following:

> The Lord God took the man and put him in the garden to till it and to keep it (Gen. 2:15).

> For you shall be in league with the stones of the field, and the wild beasts of the field shall be at peace with you (Job 5:22).

> The earth is the Lord's and the fulness thereof, the world and those who dwell therein (Ps. 24:1).

> The earth lies polluted under its inhabitants; for they have transgressed the laws, violated the statutes, broken the everlasting covenant. Therefore a curse devours the earth, and its inhabitants suffer for their guilt; therefore the inhabitants of the earth are scorched, and few men are left (Isa. 24:5-6).

> And I brought you into a plentiful land to enjoy its

[5] *Environment, Power, and Society* (New York: Wiley, 1971), p. 310.

fruits and its good things. But when you came in you defiled my land (Jer. 2:7).

And I will doubly recompense their iniquity and their sin, because they have polluted my land with the carcasses of their detestable idols (Jer. 16:18).

You shall love your neighbor as yourself (Matt. 22:39).

For whatever a man sows, that he will also reap (Gal. 6:7).

An excellent model of preaching on the theology of ecology is found in Appendix 2, pp. 98-107.

Prayer in relation to social issues may seem irrelevant to some people, who consider the popular slogan "Prayer Changes Things" to be only a pious saying. Prayer may not change *things,* but it certainly does change people. The person who prays sincerely gains insight about himself and the world in which he lives. Prayer provides a perspective on things and on what one ought to do in relating to them. A prayer by St. Francis in the sixteenth century is helping to create an ecological conscience in men today. It is a prayer for all who love the good earth.

> *Be praised, my Lord, with all your creatures,*
> *Especially Sir Brother Sun,*
> *By whom you give us the light of day!*
> *And he is beautiful and radiant with great*
>   *splendor.*
> *Of you, Most High, he is a symbol!*
>
> *Be praised, my Lord, for Brother Wind*
> *And for the Air and cloudy and clear and all*
>   *weather,*
> *By which you give sustenance to your creatures!*
>
> *Be praised, my Lord, for Sister Water,*
> *Who is very useful and humble and lovely and*
>   *chaste!*

Be praised, my Lord, for Brother Fire,
By whom you give us light at night,
And he is beautiful and merry and mighty and
    strong!

Be praised, my Lord, for our Sister Mother Earth,
Who sustains and governs us,
And produces fruits with colorful flowers and
    leaves!

                                (*Canticle of Brother Sun*)

Programming Ecological Concern

A recent survey taken among pastors and educational workers in a major Protestant denomination revealed that an overwhelming majority (81.7% of the pastors and 76.3% of the teachers) believe churches should lead their members to involve themselves in solving air and water pollution.[6] Below are some suggestions as to how churches can channel their ecological concern into concrete and constructive action.

Churches can, through their official pronouncements, help to form public opinion about moral and social issues. Some church members discount the effectiveness of such statements. Others claim that churches should never take a stand on public issues, because they have no competence to do so. Yet some of these same people support zealously the pronouncements of the church against gambling, liquor, or dancing. It is difficult to see how they can decline to support an attack on the great issues like war, racism, and ecological degradation, which threaten the lives of millions and involve the health and welfare of all mankind. A church's pronouncements on evils like these are important first of all because these problems are rooted in a theological

6 *Research Roundup*, Research and Statistics Department, Southern Baptist Sunday School Board, Nashville, Tenn., Vol. V, No. 6, Mar. 31, 1971, p. 1.

context. Furthermore, official statements provide a frame of reference for socially concerned Christians who need the support of the church; and they offer a basis and guidelines for social action programs in which individuals can participate with a sense of doing religious work.

A church may join in a community project to clean up an unsightly spot in the community. In Franklin County, Kentucky, a group of church members worked with the Audubon Society to clean up twenty miles of the Elkhorn Creek, once a beautiful stream full of bass and bluegill. Tons of trash were cleared from the stream and its banks. A church served as the headquarters for the project, and food and first aid were made available to the workers. Not only was the stream restored to a large degree of its original purity, but participation in the project brought the people of the community closer together.

A committee of concern for the environment composed of capable and well-informed persons in a church can be formed to deal with ecological problems. Many churches include scientists, government officials, educators, lawyers, and other professional persons among their members, and these would probably serve on such a committee. The committee could make a survey of the environmental problems of the community, gather facts, and suggest programs of action and specific projects.

In the midst of the ecological crisis, church members should develop a new life style of modesty and discipline. The contemporary Christian is often caught up in the acquisitive lust to enhance comfort as well as status, which, in turn, adds to the pollution problem. He falls prey to the mania for the unnecessary gadgets that are harmful to wholesome living. Too often the Christian is dominated by the values of American culture — material success, the notion of inevitable progress, and external conformity — rather than by the ethics of Christianity. The virtues of modesty, honesty, industry, and sobriety must be rediscovered.

The Christian style of life as portrayed in the New Testament is characterized by discipline: personal discipline and discipline in the family (Eph. 6:1-4), modesty in dress (I Tim. 2:9; I Pet. 3:3), self-control and godliness (Tit. 2:12). A recovery of the biblical style of life is essential not only because it is Christian, but also for the reason that it contributes to a healthy environment. If Christians persist in living by the standards of this world, they will have no distinctive life style and no model of discipline in an undisciplined society.

Since overpopulation is a major contributor to an unhealthy environment, Christians should practice discipline in regard to procreation. Christian parents should limit the number of children they have according to their ability adequately to care for them. Birth control methods are available from Planned Parenthood organizations and family welfare agencies. Love demands that parents act responsibly in the procreation as well as the rearing of children.

Conclusions

Retracing the terrain covered in this study, we may now draw some basic conclusions. There is, for one thing, overwhelming evidence that an ecological crisis does exist. The biosphere is so polluted that ecosystems are in jeopardy, forms of life are becoming extinct, and the general welfare of man is threatened. Uncontrolled population growth, untamed technology, and the exploitation of our natural resources are major causes of pollution. A plethora of panaceas are offered to save the good earth, but a massive, concerted effort on the part of all people, institutions, and governments is needed now to cope effectively with the environmental crisis.

A new ethics that extends man's responsibility beyond neighbor and society to all creation must be formulated and implemented. Love must be redefined to mean the willing of the welfare of all creatures and things.

Theology must be redefined to include a sacramental view of nature that recognizes its intrinsic worth as an object of God's redemptive purpose. At present the church has a theology of man, but not of nature, a doctrine of the salvation of the church but not of creation, an eschatology of the soul but not of the body. Ludwig Feuerbach's charge is still largely true: "Nature, the world, has no value, no interest for Christians. The Christian thinks only of himself and the salvation of his soul."[7]

From the biblical perspective, the salvation of man and nature are inseparably bound up together. Nature mourns for the manifestation of the sons of God and the glorious liberty of God's children in the new heavens and the new earth.

[7] *The Essence of Christianity* (New York: Harper, 1957), p. 287.

Appendix I

Evil and Nature

Ecological theology must come to grips with the problem of evil in nature as well as in man. Nature is a polluter along with man. Volcanoes are great polluters of the air. Volcanic activity sends millions of tons of dust into the atmosphere. Hurricanes and typhoons destroy property and may take the lives of thousands of people. Avalanches resulting from earthquakes may bury thousands of people alive.

Thousands of volumes have been written on evil in relation to man, but almost nothing on a theology of natural disasters. One can understand this shortage of material on the "evil" in nature, for it is a mystery not yet solved. As Alexander Miller declares, "the mind must do what it can with the problem," but at the same time recognize that "the solution of the mystery is not an intellectual solution, since the question is not an intellectual question."[1] Nevertheless evil is an ever present reality and man's mind must attempt to provide at least some interpretation of the problem.

[1] "Evil," in *A Handbook of Christian Theology*, ed. Marvin Halverson, *et al.* (New York: Fontana, 1966), p. 123.

The Problem of Theodicy

The problem of theodicy, that is, the vindication of God's justice in allowing evil to exist, is an ancient and perennial one. The book of Job is a classic study in theodicy. Here is a man named Job, a person of integrity and piety, who is suddenly deluged with disaster and disease. How can Job's condition be reconciled with divine justice and providence? There is no rational answer provided in the book. But every basic argument that has been made by man in connection with the problem of theodicy is touched on in Job. Some say that Job, who maintained his integrity, proved in great suffering the possibility of serving God not because he blesses one with goods, but because one really is a good person. Job's trust is revealed in his confession: "God gave, God took away. Blessed be God's name" and "Shall we accept good from God, and not accept evil?"

But Job does not reveal why nature is sometimes destructive and the cause of much human suffering. It provides no clear answer as to why God allows such disasters to occur. This was the question raised by Ralph Cudworth, professor of medicine and theology at Cambridge University, almost three hundred years ago. He observed:

> There are four possibilities with regard to evil. Either God is able and not willing to overcome it, or perchance he is not able though he may be willing. It may be that he is neither able nor willing to overcome evil. Or it remains that he is both able and willing. Only the last would seem to be worthy of a good God, and it does not happen.[2]

Cudworth gave no clear answer to this dilemma. Nor has anyone else been able to "justify the ways of God"

[2] Quoted by Charles Birch in *Nature and God* (Philadelphia: Westminster, 1965), p. 23.

in permitting natural disasters and diseases to plague mankind.

Theories of Evil

J. S. Whale has summarized the four classic answers to the problem of evil: (1) determinism or fate, which virtually makes God the author of evil; (2) the claim that the world is not intrinsically bad, since God is good. On this view, one must maintain either that evil is a delusion of the mind, or that evil is necessary to the good of the whole. The first alternative is plagued by the fact that one simply cannot get rid of the facts of greed, earthquakes, cancer, and the like by merely declaring them unreal. The second alternative once again makes God the creator of evil, and has the consequence that it would be a mistake to attempt to get rid of evil, since it is necessary for the good of the whole; (3) a form of dualism, which places the responsibility for evil on the devil. This position denies the sovereignty of God and does not satisfy the Christian; (4) the position that, since evil poses a problem for theism, one must give up theism. For atheists, the problem of evil does not arise: it is simply a fact of life, as it always has been.[3]

Whale does not deal specifically with evil in nature. He is more concerned about evil in relation to man. His basic conclusion is that the problem of evil cannot be solved in terms of an intellectual formula, but only in terms of life's experience. The Christian's answer to the problem of evil is ultimately contained in what he does with evil, "itself the result of what Christ did with evil on the Cross."[4]

C. F. D. Moule has dealt more directly with the problem of natural disasters. He raises the question as to whether *collectively* man may not be responsible for the

[3] *The Christian Answer to the Problem of Evil* (Nashville: Abingdon, 1936), Chapter I.
[4] *Ibid.,* pp. 14-15.

whole system of interlocking (animate and inanimate) movements in the world.[5] He is aware that natural disasters and diseases occurred before man appeared on earth, and that these cannot be attributed to man's disobedience or "Adam's fall." But on occasions when man is hurt or destroyed by calamities which are contrary to the will of God, he thinks that it "may be ultimately part of an almost infinitely long and subtle chain of cause and effect into which man's disobedience has entered."[6]

Moule has no answer to natural disasters occurring prior to the emergence of *homo sapiens* on earth. But he concludes that it must not be assumed that premature, sudden, and large-scale death in man or beast is always evil. Aging and merely wearing out is not intrinsically better or preferable. For the Christian faith does not view suffering and death as ultimate evils or as terminating personality.[7]

Charles Birch seeks to understand the problem of theodicy from the Christian perspective. His position is that God is not an "omnicompetent engineer" who controls the world completely in every detail, for this would take away its freedom and spontaneity.[8] Creation is the concrete realization of what is possible in the universe at different stages of development. Hence, the world is unfinished, incomplete. God's activity in the world has to do with "final causes" (purposes and values). His purposes embody what is potentially possible for the world, achieved not by mechanical intervention, but by the "persuasive lure of value and purpose."[9] God's aims and goals are achieved by struggle between disorder and the lure to completeness.

[5] *Man and Nature in the New Testament* (Philadelphia: Fortress, 1967), p. 18.
[6] *Ibid.,* p. 19.
[7] *Ibid.,* pp. 19-20.
[8] *Nature and God,* p. 102.
[9] *Ibid.,* p. 96.

For Birch, cosmic evolution involves "a fighting frontier of progressive integration" or of "persuasive love" in a universe that contains an anarchic element.[10] And where there is freedom there is also the possibility of tragedy.

Man's awareness of his own incompleteness and his struggle for fulfillment is another way of stating the "fall." The "fall" of both man and nature is a symbolic way of describing their incompleteness. The unfinishedness of the natural order is the "evil" in nature. It is simply the recognition of the consequences of spontaneity and freedom in nature.[11]

All of these theories illuminate to some degree the problem of evil. But none of them provides a rational answer to evil. Since the origin and nature of evil remain a mystery, the important factor is what one does with it.

War, racism, poverty, cruelty to children, destruction of the environment, disease, premature death, and a host of other evils result from selfishness, greed, fear, ignorance, and irresponsibility. Man must utilize his freedom to work responsibly to solve these issues.

Jesus challenged the evils of his own day and for this he was crucified. Yet he was not a victim of the cross, but the victor over death. On the cross Christ conquered the "principalities and powers," making "a public spectacle of them as captives in his victory procession" (Col. 2:15, TEV). He overcame sin and death and is alive forever. We do not see all evil removed, because all things are not yet in subjection to him. "But we see Jesus" (Heb. 2:9) and have the conviction that he will ultimately destroy all evil when he comes in glory and power at the end of the age.

Meantime the Christian's confrontation with evil is the occasion of obedience and not mere speculation

10 *Ibid.,* p. 100.
11 *Ibid.,* p. 104.

(Luke 13:4-5). Evil does not negate God's ultimate power in the universe; it spotlights man's responsibility to use his freedom and abilities to alleviate the devastation and the suffering of mankind.

Appendix II

The Theology of Ecology

A Sermon by John R. Claypool

Scripture Reference: Romans 8:18-23

Two years ago I am not even sure I had heard the word "ecology," and I certainly did not realize the gigantic proportion of the problems this word stands for. Since then, however, we have all been inundated about what may happen very shortly to this planet earth; and whether we like it or not, we have to make some kind of response to all of this. It is part of the mission of the church that she should be involved with you in such an endeavor, which is why we are offering this particular emphasis at this time. It is appropriate both to our spiritual and historical lives, and in this sermon I would like to set the stage for what is to follow by trying to put the issue in as clear a perspective as possible.

The ecological problem, as I see it, is basically one of man's relationship to the various support systems of the world on which he depends for his life; specifically, the air, the earth, and the water. Both in quantity and in quality, this relationship is in trouble, which is why the dire threats of suffocation and starvation in the immediate future are being made. Perhaps we can grasp it more readily if I try to scale it down and illustrate it by something I once personally witnessed happening.

It occurred to a farmer in middle Tennessee who fixed up a dwelling on his place to house the tenant who was to work for him. This farmer went far beyond what many did in that area, for he saw to it that the house was not only wired amply for electricity, but he also installed a water system at no little expense that included a large cistern and inside plumbing. He "made a trade" as they put it in that community, and the new employee moved in, and right away my friend had his first misgivings, for the man turned out to have more children and relatives living with him than the farmer expected, and from the first, the five-room house was badly overcrowded. Two days after they moved, the owner was called and told that the water system had stopped working, only to find that the tenants had let the faucets run indiscriminately, and the whole cistern had been used up. Three nights later the house burned to the ground, and it was subsequently discovered that the electrical system had been overloaded by too many appliances. I remember standing in front of the remains of that house with the farmer as he expressed both his frustration and anger. "This was a decent place to live — a workable set-up — and look what they have gone and done. With a little judgment and insight, a family could have lived here for decades."

That scene comes to my mind when I hear of ecological problems, for here in tiny microcosm were some of the same dynamics. For example, part of the difficulty in this situation was a quantitative one — there were simply too many people trying to live in too small a space and off too few resources. No wonder that the water system and the energy system gave way. And of course, this same factor is basic to so many of our environmental problems today. There are simply too many people trying to inhabit this spaceship called earth. The medical revolution that has made it possible for more people to be born and survive and live longer now threatens to turn on itself and destroy all life. The population explosion, unless somehow brought under control, will cause every problem we have so to escalate that they will be unmanageable. The quantity question, then — to my farmer friend and to the world — is basic.

But there was also a qualitative dimension to this little tragedy that cannot be ignored. This tenant family did not try to understand the support systems which made that house the livable unit it was, and out of such understanding to collaborate with them. Rather, they arrogantly acted as if their desires were the only factor to be considered. They never thought of a cistern that held only so much water or wires that could carry only so much electricity. It was as if these things were looked on as so much "stuff" to be treated any way they pleased, and thus the problem. They found out too late that these support systems had a life and structure of their own, and that they could strike back when abused. The same thing can be said about our treatment of the universe and its many support systems. We have related to the air and the earth and the water pretty much like those tenants related to the cistern and the electric wires, and this is why the whole thing is starting to collapse all around us. The quality of our relation here — that is, thinking we were all that mattered and that the universe has no life or structure of its own — has been our undoing.

To talk like this is to take a page straight out of the Bible, for if you look at the early chapters of Genesis, this is exactly the perspective you will encounter there. This world is pictured as being fashioned by a joyful Creator, and — to use a modern slang expression — this Creator really knew how "to put it all together." While what we have in Genesis are not scientific essays but religious poems, nonetheless they depict how master-fully everything fits together and works hand-in-hand with all else. There is an incredible balance between the various aspects of nature. For example, we humans need oxygen to survive, and we inhale this from the atmosphere and exhale carbon dioxide. However, many forms of plant life need carbon dioxide to live, and they inhale it and exhale oxygen. This is but one example of the fantastic balance built into the way God put it all together, and Genesis indicates that man's place was to be a knowing partner in this finely balanced process. He was called on to name the animals; that is, to understand their structures and penetrate the mystery of their lives, and then to collaborate with them in a reciprocity that flowed back and forth. Man was part of the animals' and plants' support system, just as they were part of his, and so life was to be.

However, Genesis records that a breakdown occurred in all this, and it pinpoints the problem with man and his refusal to be himself and to plan the part he was meant to play. Instead of being an insightful collaborator with all these support systems, man decided to assume the stance of an arrogant manipulator. Just like those mindless tenants, he refused to learn the "names" of what supported him, and chose rather to treat them any way he wanted to. As a result, all creation was thrown out of kilter, and instead of being collaborators together, everything assumed an adversary role — man began to have to battle his mate and brother and the animals and the earth and everything. The root cause here is this quality of relation we have spoken of earlier, and it is the poison spring that contaminated all else.

This attitude of mindless arrogance toward the physical universe is why we have come to such an ecological impasse. By not realizing that the air and the earth and the water have lives and structures of their own and cannot be treated any way we please, we have seriously disrupted the balance of life and imperiled our survival. For example, by wiping out vast areas of plant life and covering them with inert concrete, or defoliating large segments of greenery so we can kill the enemy better, we have threatened the oxygen-carbon dioxide balance and could well wind up suffocating. Or again, by dumping indiscriminate amounts of waste into our rivers and oceans we have unsettled the vital processes there. Lake Erie is today like a tank of poisonous chemicals, and many say it is a prophecy of what all our bodies of water will become.

On and on I could go, but the evidence is clear. We are in big trouble with our environment — bigger trouble than we have known — and the problem is our human relation to the support systems of the air and the earth and the water on which our survival depends. In terms of quantity and quality, we are in trouble, and the question arises: what are we going to do about it? In light of this apocalyptic sword of Damocles hanging over our future, what response are we going to make?

Some people with great faith in man's rational power say: *get out the facts.* Tell people the situation! The problem, they feel, is basically one of ignorance, and if man can just be apprised of the situation and how he got into these straits and what the consequences are, then he surely will adapt and find ways to solve the problems. And I, for one, would not want to underestimate what this approach can accomplish. After all, our Lord himself recognized that much of the evil of life is rooted in blindness as well as in badness, and thus prayed from the cross: "Father, forgive them, for they know not what they do." Surely it is important that the alarm be sounded and that the facts be disseminated, for we would not even be as aware as we are now of this threat were it not for heralds of truth like Rachel Carson and many others.

Yet having said that, I must confess a real doubt of my own that information alone is going to be our salvation here. The problem is that man is not just a rational creature for whom knowing is the same as doing. He is, in fact, a complex creature of many facets, like, for example, emotions, fears, defenses, habits and other things. And for this reason getting men to change radically, even when their own self-interest is at stake, can be extraordinarily difficult. The way most people have responded to the link-up between tobacco and lung cancer is a revealing case in point. The evidence is now overwhelming that excessive smoking, particularly of cigarettes, is hazardous to health. Yet I know many people who do not contest this fact at all, but go right on smoking and intend to do so even if it means cancer and a shorter life.

And this is a side of the problem we have to face in terms of the ecological situation. It is not just a question of information or education for the simple reason that man is more than a mind. There is a darkness deeper down in us than that of not knowing. It is the darkness of not wanting to be, of not wanting to live, of not wanting to grapple with existence as it is given to us in freedom and responsibility.

I am deeply impressed by the question Jesus asked the lame man who had lain helpless for thirty-eight years by the pool of Bethesda: "Do you want to be healed?" (John 5:6). On the surface that may sound like a ridiculous question, for we naively assume that everyone wants to be well and never sick. But Jesus realized it was not that simple. You see, paradoxical as it may sound, sickness has its own strange consolations. To be sick is to be exempt from responsibility and complex decision-making. It is to be taken care of instead of having to care for another. And after a while, it can become a habit, a way of life. Take this man by the pool for example. Thirty-eight years is a long time, and having grown accustomed to certain routines, a change, even back to health, would have involved costly adjustments. This is why Jesus was so right in asking the question: "Do you really want to be healed?" He meant by this: are you prepared to change and accept the new challenges of health? Are you willing to pay the price that must be paid if healing becomes a reality?

I contend this is the question facing all of us as far as ecology is concerned. Do we really want to be healed? That is what we have to ponder, and we need to think about what it involves. A simplistic "yes" may not truly represent the way we really feel about this matter.

For example, wanting to be healed means admitting openly and honestly that there is a problem and that we are sick and are partly at fault. Some of the hardest words a human being ever has to utter are: "I am wrong. I have sinned. I have made a mistake." And our capacities for denial and evasion here are massive. In fact, I know many people right now who refuse to believe there is an ecological crisis, and dismiss it as another Communist plot or a fad that is soon to pass again. Our ability to choose fantasy over actuality and accept only what we want to be true runs very deep, and this is part of what has to be faced in wanting to be healed. We have to have reality-perception enough and courage enough to admit: we are sick. We are ecological sinners. We are at fault.

Another facet of being healed is a willingness to become involved in the cure and not expect it to be done for us without any cost or effort. There is a childishness that likes to sit and wait and have some super-power solve all his problems for him. In religious terms, this is called "quietism," and can be seen in the people who say: "God must do it all. We are to wait, sit passively, and let Him intervene." While there are probably millions like this, there are even more whom I would call "secular quietists"; that is, they do not expect God to intervene, but they do expect our vaunted technology to come up with some innovation that will solve all of this without any pain. You have heard people talk of the mythical "they" — "they" will come up with this or that, and pretty soon all will be well. And as a result we do not have to change a thing, but can go right on as we are. Really wanting to be healed is putting aside this kind of childishness and recognizing that because we are the ones who are sick and have made ourselves sick, we must be involved painfully in any cure. A theme that runs through all the Bible is the assertion that "without the shedding of blood there is no remission of sin," and this means that salvation or healing always involves suffering or it never happens.

And right here is where I have my greatest uneasiness about all of us and this question of healing the ecological wound that runs so deep. What is going to have to change is our style of life, the way we have become accustomed to living and consuming and acting. Are we willing to adapt at the level? The Good Life — however vaguely it may be defined — has most of us securely in its clutches, and this glut of affluence is one of the main culprits to our environment. Do you realize that in 1969 our country alone produced 48 billion cans and 28 billion bottles to be disposed of, to say nothing of the 7 million cars that had to be junked and the 142 billion tons of pollution we emptied into the air? It is estimated that the average American is anywhere from 25 to 500 times as destructive of his environment as the average Indian peasant, which is why the ecological night of total extinction may well come to America first. These are the apocalyptic facts, and Jesus' question is the real issue: "Do we want to be healed?" Which means, are we willing to undergo the radical alteration of life style that will be called for if the balance of man and air and earth and water is to be restored? Nothing less than this will really touch the depths of the prob-

lem. Yet, nothing could be harder than to get people
to change what they have grown accustomed to having
and spending and consuming.

I must admit that I fluctuate between pessimism and
optimism at this point. At times I have very little hope,
for I realize how deeply ingrained our habits are and
that nothing is harder to alter than habit. As the *Three-penny Opera* puts it:

> *For even saintly folk will act like sinners*
> *Unless they have their customary dinners.*

And this is not just other people's problems, this is a
problem for me personally. In preparing this sermon,
I was forced to ask: what real change have you made in
your life style since learning of the ecological crisis?
We have changed soap powder, take shorter showers and
try to buy lead-free gas, but I still have two eight-cylin-
der cars, have done nothing to work for mass transit
systems, still buy plastic milk cartons, and have yet to
write that first public official in either support or dis-
agreement. If I am to do my part in the healing, one
hundred times more radicality than I have shown thus
far is going to be called for. And while a few are doing
more, I do not see many people aroused, and thus my
pessimism. Are we willing to pay the price?

But then I pick up the Bible and read in Romans
how "the whole creation waits in eager longing for the
revealing of the sons of God . . ."; how "all creation is
groaning in travail together" until at last it is "freed
from the bondage of decay" and "obtains the glorious
liberty of the children of God." And then some optimism rises in me, for I realize that God is on the side
of health and wholeness and is at work for good in all
this as he always has been. This does not mean he is
going to do everything for us so that without any pain
or effort what is crooked will come straight. Even for
God, "without the shedding of blood there is no remis-

sion of sin." But it does mean that we are not alone in our efforts. The promise of God applies to ecology; if we will confess our sin, he will do something in faithfulness and justice to forgive us our sins and cleanse us from all unrighteousness. If we will just be sons of God with all the responsibility and freedom that implies, things could be different.

There is hope, then, but it is not automatic. We do not *have to be* saved in this area or in any other. It is the ultimate dignity of man to decide finally whether he wants to be healed or not healed, or more profoundly, whether he wants to live or to die. I talk occasionally with people who are threatening suicide, and while I do everything in my power to persuade them against it, I remind them that the choice finally is theirs. To live or not to live, and how one shall live, these are decisions no one can make for another. Which is where the question of ecology finally leads. I am convinced we can be healed and save both the earth and ourselves, but in order for this to happen, we have to want to be healed and to be willing to undergo the treatment that this involves. And to want to be healed means you must want to live and not die.

So the question is: do we want to live? Deuteronomy pictures Moses as standing before Israel for the last time and saying: "I call heaven and earth to witness this day, that I have set before you life and death, the blessing and curse. Therefore, choose life" (30:19). This remains the challenge to every generation, and to us.

Well?

Appendix III

Environmental Societies

There are hundreds of societies and groups seeking to save the good earth. While their programs vary and their methods differ, their goal is the same: to conserve our natural resources and to improve our quality of life. Some of these societies are listed below.

American Forestry Association, 919 17th St., N.W., Washington, D.C. 20006.

Appalachian Trail Conference, 1718 N. St., N.W., Washington, D.C. 20036.

Conservation Education Association, 1250 Connecticut Ave., N.W., Washington, D.C. 20036.

Friends of Earth, 451 Pacific Ave., San Francisco, Calif. 94133.

National Association of Soil and Water Conservation Districts, 1025 Vermont Ave., N.W., Washington, D.C. 20005.

National Audubon Society, 1130 Fifth Avenue, New York, N.Y. 10038.

National Parks Association, 1701 18th St., N.W., Washington, D.C. 20009.

National Wildlife Federation, 1412 16th St., N.W., Washington, D.C.

Planned Parenthood, 515 Madison Ave., New York, N.Y. 10022.

Resources for the Future, 1145 19th St., N.W., Washington, D.C. 20006.

Sierra Club, 1050 Mills Tower, San Francisco, Calif. 94104.

Urban America, 1717 Massachusetts Ave., N.W., Washington, D.C. 20036.

The Wilderness Society, 729 15th St., N.W., Washington, D.C. 20005.

Appendix IV

Eco-Films

Films dealing with the environmental problem are available from federal and state agencies, commercial distributors, colleges, universities, local libraries, and private organizations. A rental charge or fee is required by most of them. In some cases the films can be purchased. Films directly related to this study are listed below.

The Poisoned Air. 50 min., color, sound.

From American Documentary Films, 336 W. 84th Street, New York, N.Y. 10024 and 379 Bay Street, San Francisco, Calif. 94133.

The Food Crisis. 60 min., black and white, sound.
USA: Seeds of Change. 30 min., black and white, sound.
Multiply and Subdue the Earth. 67 min., black and white, sound.

From Audio-Visual Center, Indiana University, Bloomington, Indiana 47401.

No Room for Wilderness? 28 min., color, sound.
The Redwoods. 30 min., color, sound.

From Association Films, 600 Grand Ave., Ridgefield, New Jersey 07657.

The Cars in Your Life. 30 min., color, sound.
City of Necessity. 30 min., color, sound.

From Contemporary Films, Princeton Road, Hights-
town, New Jersey 08520 and Evanston, Illinois
60202.

The Stuff We Throw Away. 22 min., color, sound.
5,000 Dumps. 21 min., color, sound.
The Realities of Recycling. 38 min., color, sound.

All free from National Medical Audiovisual Center,
Station K, Atlanta, Ga. 30324.

The Time of Man. 50 min., color, sound.

From The American Museum of Natural History,
Central Park West at 79th St., New York, N.Y.
10024.

Who Killed Lake Erie? 51 min., color, sound.
The Noise Boom. 26 min., color, sound.

Check with your state universities for these films.

Appendix V

Bibliography

A. Scientific and Sociological Studies

Barbour, Ian G. *Science and Secularity: the Ethics of Technology.* New York: Harper, 1970.

Baron, Robert A. *The Tyranny of Noise.* New York: St. Martin, 1970.

Borland, Hal, *et al. Crisis of Survival.* New York: Morrow, 1970.

Cailliet, Greg, *et al. Everyman's Guide to Ecological Living.* New York: Macmillan, 1971.

Carson, Rachel. *Silent Spring.* New York: Crest, 1969.

Commoner, Barry. *Science and Survival.* New York: Viking, 1966.

—————. *The Closing Circle.* New York: Knopf, 1971.

Dansereau, Pierre, ed. *Challenge for Survival: Land, Air, and Water for Man in Megalopolis.* New York: Columbia U. P., 1970.

Davis, Wayne. *Readings in Human Population Ecology.* Englewood Cliffs, N. J.: Prentice-Hall, 1971.

DeBell, Garrett. *The Environmental Handbook.* New York: Ballantine, 1970.

Detwyler, Thomas. *Man's Impact on Environment.* New York: McGraw-Hill, 1971.

✓Disch, Robert, ed. *The Ecological Conscience: Values for Survival*. Englewood Cliffs, N. J.: Prentice-Hall, 1970.

Earth Day — The Beginning: A Guide for Survival. Compiled and edited by the National Staff of Environmental Action. New York: Bantam, 1970.

Ehrlich, Paul and Anne. *Population, Resources, Environment: Issues in Human Ecology*. San Francisco: Freeman, 1970.

Graham, Frank. *Since Silent Spring*. New York: Houghton-Mifflin, 1970.

Grossman, Mary, and John Hamlet. *Our Vanishing Wilderness*. New York: Grosset and Dunlap, 1969.

Leopold, Aldo. *Sand County Almanac*. New York: Oxford U. P., 1949.

Marx, Wesley. *The Frail Ocean*. New York: Ballantine, 1969.

McHarg, Ian. *Design with Nature*. New York: Doubleday, 1969.

Mitchell, John, and Constance Stallings, eds. *Ecotactics*. New York: Pocket Books, 1970.

Odum, Eugene. *Ecology*. New York: Holt, Rinehart and Winston, 1969.

Odum, Howard T. *Environment, Power, and Society*. New York: Wiley, 1971.

Paddock, William and Paul. *Famine 1975! America's Decision: Who Will Survive?* Boston: Little-Brown, 1967.

Shepard, Paul, and Daniel McKinley, eds. *The Subversive Science*. New York: Houghton-Mifflin, 1968.

Still, Henry. *Quest for Quiet*. Harrisburg, Pa.: Stackpole Books, 1970.

Van Sickle, Dirch. *The Ecological Citizen*. New York: Harper, 1971.

B. Religious Studies

Bonifazi, Conrad. *A Theology of Things*. Philadelphia: Lippincott, 1967.

Buber, Martin. *I and Thou*. Edinburgh: T. & T. Clark, 1944.

Cox, Harvey. *The Secular City*. New York: Macmillan, 1965.

Demant, V. A. *The Idea of a Natural Order*. Philadelphia: Fortress, 1966.

Elder, Frederick. *Crisis in Eden.* Nashville: Abingdon, 1970.

Moule, C. F. D. *Man and Nature in the New Testament.* Philadelphia: Fortress, 1967.

Niebuhr, H. Richard. *The Responsible Self.* New York: Harper, 1963.

Raven, Charles E. *Natural Religion and Christian Theology.* Cambridge: The University Press, 1953.

Richardson, Herbert W. *Toward an American Theology.* New York: Harper, 1967.

Rust, Eric. *Nature and Man in Biblical Thought.* London: Lutterworth, 1953.

————. *Nature — Garden or Desert?* Waco, Tex.: Word, 1971.

Santmire, Paul. *Brother Earth.* New York: Nelson, 1970.

Teilhard de Chardin, Pierre. *The Phenomenon of Man.* New York: Harper, 1965.

————. *Man's Place in Nature.* New York: Harper, 1966.

————. *The Divine Milieu.* New York: Harper, 1960.

Temple, William. *Nature, Man and God.* London: Macmillan, 1953.

Tillich, Paul. *Theology of Culture.* New York: Oxford U. P., 1959.